Raymond Castrogiovanni

Reincarnation

Past Lives Revisited

Reincarnation : Past Lives Revisited by Raymond Castrogiovanni ©

Reprint 2013

I should like to express my appreciation to the following for the production of this book. To my family for their encouragement; to my friend and colleague, Clare Francis and my son Daniel, for interpreting my hand writing and translating it into readable English; to all those brave souls who shared their experiences and whose names have been changed in some instances to protect identities.

ISBN 1492392715

Widow's Sonnet

I lay sleepless upon the scent of you.

Hugging and caressing that favored shirt.

Where, like loving doves, we would kiss and coo.

My breast heaves, though my heart does greatly hurt.

In darkness I lay, no comfort at night.

'O coldness; hotness, the torment won't die.

I pray this ends and come the morning light.

Lonely stillness aches my endless goodbye.

Perfume still pleases from the rose yellow,

I held so tightly before it was cast.

Each night I dream petals on my pillow.

Beautiful, the rose dreamt at my breast.

I feel your soulful kiss on my shoulder.

Please stay with me (dear spirited) lover.

Ghost Sonnet

They say I'm at peace, in a better place.
If this be true, why do I yearn your kiss?
Each night I am gladdened, seeing your face.
When you wish for me, I'm with you, 'O bliss'.
I watched you as you dropped a rose,
Unseen was I, amid tearful mourners.
Worry not, for that wake was not my close.
Please, don't cry, for you are too beautiful.
So for now I will stay with you awhile,
and into your ear I gently whisper
Sweet love dreams that bring to your lips a smile.
Thus I conjure rose petals for your hair.
Each time you weep, I cry in sorrow.
Though you know it not, we have tomorrow.

Contents

Part One

Introduction   *10*

Past Life Regression Techniques   *13*

Exercises To Access Past Lives   *21*

The Language Of Reincarnation   *31*

Part Two

Peter's Story   *36*

Barbara's Story   *54*

Linda's Story   *74*

Alan's Story   *89*

Jenny's Story   *108*

Darragh's Story   *138*

Marine's Story   *164*

Luke's Story   *187*

Epilogue   *213*

Part One

Introduction

Reincarnation The Cycle of Lives

Karma The sum of a person's actions in previous states of existence, viewed as deciding his or her fate in future existences; destiny. Oxford English Dictionary

Karma is perhaps the most misunderstood word and yet understanding it is perhaps quite simple. Let us not look for a definition; but instead let us look for the spirit in the word.

Karmic ideals crop up everywhere in commonsense, the ideal of 'judge and ye shall be judged', 'do unto others as you would have them do unto you', 'you only get out what you put in', 'to give is better than to receive', 'the truth will out', the list is endless. I suppose what I am saying is that Karma may be a chance to put right some wrong deed in a past life; but it is more likely to be a set of conditions to be overcome in your life to help the personal growth of your soul.

When I question people on Karma or the idea of past-lives, the usual response is to define it as some sort of consequence for past ill deeds, or some form of reward for the good done in a past life. Frequently there is the humorous response: "I must have been a terrible person last time, to have to put up with my present life!" Would that it were so simple. A fundamental query in relation to this is whether there is actually a tangible connection between a previous life and a present life.

I would suggest that sometimes there is the weak possibility of such a link, but in the main there is not. An example of this link can be an unreasonable fear or phobia, birthmarks, or a persistent memory that does not in any way belong to this life. There are numerous anecdotal stories that support this theory, such as small children who in their infantile innocence make quite remarkable statements such as, "I had a different mummy before I lived here", or when travelling into an area they have never been to before, becoming quite familiar and excited, perhaps stating, "That's where I used to live," or possibly remarking on experiences they could not have encountered in their own, new and brief lives, such as: "When I was a mum I had three children, but we all got sick". What is remarkable with most people I speak to, is that they all seem to have one of these stories, where their child has made strange, inexplicable claims, yet in the main people dismiss them as cute, childish ramblings.

Amongst Buddhists, Hindus and several other religions these stories or remembrances are treated differently, especially amongst North Indian and Tibetan communities. To them, the acceptance of reincarnation is not just a religious ideal, but a way of life. When a Dalai Lama dies, Tibetan priests search out infant boys in the villages and towns for their new Dalai Lama, to be reincarnated into one of these children. Great pains are taken to ensure the correct choice is made. A lovely story about the present Dalai Lama tells of how, when he was a toddler, a priest had visited his parents' house wearing beads that had belonged to the deceased Dalai Lama. On seeing the beads the boy child pulled at them and repeatedly said "Mine, mine".

Another well-documented story tells of a poor Indian family whose daughter remembers being shot dead in a previous life, as a young shopkeeper with a wife and children. The girl was able to talk in detail about an actual village from another province, as well as discuss the geography of the place; eventually the girl's family and the shopkeeper's family managed to meet, subsequently becoming good friends. This friendship may have been cemented by the money and jewellery which was found by the girl, that had been secretly hidden by the shopkeeper before his death. Anecdotes like these are numerous. So in this book I set out to help you experience some past lives of others, whilst also offering a safe and easy-to-follow method to access past lives.

Past Life Regression Techniques

Heart, Light, Harmony State

The Heart, Light Harmony State is arrived at through meditation, using rose quartz crystal. This technique allows us to open the heart chakra and crown chakra, creating a link between them and opening a channel to past lives.

During some forms of meditation or hypnosis, REM (Rapid Eye Movement) can occur. This is the state of altered awareness. It looks very like sleep to the observer and the analogy is often used. Even the common name for this state, hypnosis, means sleep-like state.

To enable you to understand and work the Heart, Light, Harmony State method, there is an exercise in this book which will be easier to follow than you might imagine. However, before we get there, it is important to discuss meditation, the aura and the chakras, along with information on rose quartz crystal.

The Aura

This is an electromagnetic energy field that surrounds the body, and is sometimes perceived by sensitive people and clairvoyants. Today, through Kirlian photography, even sceptics are able to see the wonderful colours emanating from the body. Though invisible to the naked eye, there are occasions when people who have no experience of psychic perception sometimes see colours around an individual during a performance, lecture, or stressful event. During pregnancy, the aura can be particularly bright (hence the common expression "she's glowing").

The depth, density, colour and movement can vary a great deal. A simple example is when we are in good health and everything is right with the world, the aura will tend to glow bright colours, and be so large it can extend up to two meters around us.

The other extreme is when we feel sad or depressed, in poor health or fearful, then the aura shrinks, loses its colour, or shows itself in murky colours. Most of us, however, are somewhere in between, although there are times in life when we experience all of the above. But for the purpose of this exercise, we will use positive visualisation to help us manipulate the colours in our aura, for example: colour breathing.

Chakras

Sanskrit: Spinning wheel

The chakra signifies one of seven basic energy centres within and outside the body. Each of these centres correlates to major nerve ganglia, having their origin in the spinal column. In addition, the chakras correlate to levels of consciousness, archetypal elements, developmental stages of life, colours, sounds, body functions and much more besides.

The Seven Major Chakras

Chakra One *Earth, physical identity, oriented to self preservation.*
This is known as the base chakra and is located at the base of the spine (this is the centre of lowest vibration). It represents the earth element, the colour red, and is associated with our survival instincts, and to our sense of grounding and the connection of our bodies to the physical plane. Ideally,

this chakra brings us health, prosperity, security and dynamic presence.

Chakra Two *Water, emotional identity, oriented to self-gratification.*
This is known as the sacral chakra and is located midway between the pelvis and the navel, and is associated with the lower back and sexual organs. It is connected with the element water, with emotions and sexuality; the colour associated with it is orange. It allows us to connect with others through feeling, desire, sensation and movement. Ideally this chakra brings us fluidity and grace, depth of feeling, sexual fulfillment and the ability to accept change.

Chakra Three *Fire, ego identity, oriented to self definition.*
This is the solar plexus chakra, the power chakra, and is located approximately three inches below the base of the sternum (breastbone). The colour is yellow. It rules our personal power, will and autonomy, as well as our metabolism. When healthy, this chakra brings us energy, effectiveness, spontaneity and non-dominating power.

Chakra Four *Air, social identity, oriented to self-acceptance.*
This is the heart chakra and is located approximately three inches above the sternum, in the centre of the chest, and is the middle chakra in the system of seven. It is related to love, and is the integrator of opposites in the psyche: mind and body, male and female, persona and shadow, ego and unity. The colour associated with it is green. A healthy fourth chakra allows us to love deeply, feel compassion, have a deep sense of peace and centredness.

Chakra Five *Sound, creative identity, oriented to self-expression.*

This chakra is the throat chakra and is thus related to communication and creativity. The colour is blue. Here we experience the world symbolically through vibration, such as the vibration of sound representing language.

Chakra Six *Light, archetypal identity, oriented to self-reflection.*

This is known as the third eye chakra and is located at the centre of the forehead, between the brows. The colour is indigo. It is related to the act of seeing, both physically and intuitively, and as such it opens our psychic faculties and our understanding of archetypal levels. When healthy it allows us to see clearly, in effect, letting us 'see the big picture'.

Chakra Seven *Thought, universal identity, oriented to self-knowledge.*

This is the crown chakra and is positioned at the crown of the head. This chakra was depicted as a halo by artists from the early middle ages. It may have led to the origin of the tonsure (the part of the hair cut away in a circle on priests, monks and friars). The colour is violet, or sometimes golden light. This relates to consciousness as pure awareness. It is our connection to the greater world beyond, to a timeless, spaceless place of all-knowing. This chakra has the highest vibration, and is considered to be the most spiritual. When developed it brings us knowledge, wisdom, understanding, spiritual connection and bliss.

Most people do know what it feels like when a chakra is suddenly activated either through stress or excitement. For example, fear can be felt as 'butterflies' in the stomach (or in other words the fast spinning of the sacral chakra). A further example is when on a roller-coaster ride, some people experience a tingling in the base of the spine. Yet another example occurs when your stomach jumps when encountering the love of your life. This is the solar plexus chakra opening in reaction to the body's happiness.

Conversely, the stomach can churn when you instinctively feel that something bad is about to happen. The feelings described for the solar plexus chakra can equally apply to the heart chakra. The throat chakra is a little more subtle. Occasionally, when out of balance, the voice is lost for a short period, and people with persistent throat problems may have an imbalanced throat chakra.

The third eye chakra deals with the psychic realms and dreams, and is less likely to cause any physical sensation.

The crown chakra can sometimes react with a tightening of the scalp, and goose pimples going through the body. Some people, when experiencing powerful healing techniques, can feel the crown chakra literally burning.

Most people have experienced some of these sensations from time to time. However, during the exercise you will be carrying out, you are unlikely to record such strong physical responses, as the exercise is about relaxation, although some other techniques involve the stimulation of the third eye chakra.

For the purpose of the exercise, the chakras which will be focused on will be the heart and the crown chakras. By linking these two together, we drop the consciousness from the head to the heart. This may sound bizarre, but it will work!

Rose Quartz Crystal

This is a pink, usually translucent stone, sometimes called the 'love stone'. Rose quartz is found in rock as masses, duruses, granular structures, grains, veins and, rarely, as crystal structures.

The colours range from deep pink to a soft pink, almost a golden white. It is a popular stone with jewellers and healers alike.

Its main property for healing includes calming the heart, as a cure for love-sickness, to help with anxiety states, to induce calmness during stressful periods and to boost self-esteem.

Rose quartz becomes a useful tool in opening the heart chakra, and through meditation and the linking of the crown chakra we are able to experience past lives.

Meditation and Colour Breathing

To undergo the process of the exercise described in this book, to access past lives, a meditation breathing technique is needed.

A simple 2/2 rhythm helps achieve a good relaxed breathing pattern. To begin make sure there will be no distractions. Switch off all phones and make sure you choose a time when you will not be disturbed. Give yourself at least ten minutes to practice your breathing technique.

Seat yourself well into, but comfortably upon, a dining chair. Hold your back straight, with hands held lightly together, one on top of the other at your chest. It is best to remove shoes, tights, or socks and place your bare feet flat on the floor.

Close your eyes and take a long, deep breath. Inhale through the nose to the count of two; then release your breath at your own pace through your open mouth. Continue to do this until you become relaxed and your rhythm is even. You may find your personal rhythm is slightly different from the 2/2 rhythm, but it should be fairly close to this.

The next thing to do is imagine a bright colour around you (when we do the exercise the colour we use will be pink) but for now choose your favourite colour - not black. It is important the colour is light and bright. Personally, I like to use an amethyst purple or an emerald green.

Now that you imagine your favourite colour, see it in your mind's eye as a translucent cloud around you. As you breath in, imagine you take the cloud colour deep into your lungs. You can enhance this by imagining a scent or aroma to the colour. For example, lavender for purple; menthol for green; strawberries for red; roses for pink and so on.

As you breathe out, visualise your exhaled breath as a murky grey, taking away all the negative energy inside you. After some moments you will notice in your visualisation that your exhaled breath becomes as bright and colourfully clear as the cloud you inhale.

At this point, take a deep breath in and hold this to the count of four, and then in your mind's eye breath out clear breath. You are now holding the colour you generated at your heart chakra, and hopefully you will feel the benefit of the energy within the colour you chose.

Exercises To Access Past Lives

It is best to work with a trustworthy friend, someone you feel relaxed with. They will be helpful as a prompt to aid you with the breathing exercises, visualisation, and for questioning you in your altered state, as well as to record the proceedings. After numerous sessions, you may feel confident enough to go through the procedure on your own.

What You Need

Time

(allow yourself at least one hour)

A Recording device

A pen and paper

A piece of rose quartz crystal

(the size is immaterial)

Exercise to Achieve an Altered State of Awareness

Sit on a dining chair, place your bare feet flat on the floor, keep your back straight, holding the piece of rose quartz in your left hand, at your heart chakra, with your right hand gently clasped into the left.

Now close your eyes and begin to breathe in rhythm, in through your nose, hold to the count of two; then out through your open mouth. As you do so, focus your thoughts on the rose quartz.

In your mind's eye see it glowing and infusing the atmosphere around you with it's colour, so your aura becomes a beautiful, translucent pink.

Continue to breathe in rhythm until your exhaled breath expels all the negative energy from your body, and you are completely surrounded by a glowing pink aura.

Now take a deep breath in and hold to the count of four, then exhale clear, pure breath.

You are now holding the energy of the rose quartz at your heart chakra, which is now spinning open. You may feel something, but if you do not, rest assured at this point your heart chakra is open.

The next step is to drop your consciousness so that your heart chakra is open. This happens automatically when you begin to focus your mind on the quest in hand.

In your mind's eye see yourself slowly walking into a forest. As you go deeper into the forest you feel the warmth, it is a sunny day. There is an easy path that you are following and on this gentle path there lies a large and ornate golden key. You pick the key up and carry on your journey through the woods.

Next you come to a clearing, where the wood is separated by a sparkling stream. You cross the stream by stepping stones, and when you reach the other side there is a small, rose-covered cottage. The key you are carrying exactly fits the lock to the cottage door.

You go inside and discover the pretty cottage is well furnished, bright and clean. You seem to instinctively know that no one is there. You glance around and notice a chair that appears to be the most comfortable you have ever seen, so you feel invited to sit down and relax.

Once seated comfortably, your eyes skim across the room and notice a full length oval mirror. You look into the mirror expecting to see your reflection. However, the mirror image is blurred, out of focus.

But as you continue to stare into the mirror, the image gradually becomes clear. However, the reflection, even though you know it is you, has changed. The reflection looks different and is also dressed differently. As you look, speak out the images you see.

Look deeper into the background; a change begins to happen. Your consciousness, as well as being there in your chair, is also in the reflection and you are able to experience the life of the image you are seeing.

This experience may last just a few seconds, but it can seem like a lifetime. The session may come to a natural conclusion, or you may choose to end the session yourself. To do this, simply open your eyes.

Either way, sit quietly and breathe steadily for a few moments before you stand up. If after your first attempt little happens, do not be discouraged, as practice will improve your ability to achieve the Heart, Light, Harmony State.

Some people are able to record numerous past lives, and some only one or two. To get the best from a past life experience, try to record as much information as you can (this is why it is very helpful to work with a partner). If not, then do so as soon as possible after returning to a normal state of awareness.

Deep Relaxation Technique

This is an alternative method you can use to achieve an altered state of awareness. This works very well if you are alone, but it is more practical to have a friend with you during the session so that they can record or report back what you say, and also operate the relaxation tape which I am going to tell you to record for this purpose. I would suggest you read and re-read this method and then when you understand it, dictate it onto a cassette tape so that you can play it to go through the process.

It is important you choose a place and time when you will not be disturbed. Switch 0f all the phones you have. Choose a comfortable chair, and make sure the room is warm enough, as your body temperature will fall as time goes on. You may need a blanket and some woolly socks.

Make sure you allow sufficient time to go through your session. It is best not to undergo this when you are tired (as you will most likely fall asleep!) or if you are feeling unwell, for obvious reasons.

After recording the initial part of this method, follow on by recording the wake-up technique for when you want to return from your journey. Your friend can play it at the appropriate time.

Method

It is important that you use your voice as a tool here. When you record this text, lower your voice slightly, speak softly, gently but clearly, and with authority.

"Lie back in the chair

Look upwards and backwards at a point of your own choosing on the ceiling

Keep looking at that point

Focus. Do not let your eyes wander

Start counting slowly backwards, from ten

Say it mentally in your head, not out loud

Count… slowly… in rhythm… continue counting

As you count, let yourself go completely limp and loose

While you are counting you can feel your eyes becoming very, very tired

They are a bit watery, the point on the ceiling is looking a bit blurred

Ten… relax

Nine… breathe slowly and deeply

Eight… you are becoming more relaxed

Seven… relax, more relaxed

Six… deeper and deeper

Five… breathe slowly and deeply

Four… you are feeling more relaxed

Three… deeper and deeper

Two… very relaxed

One… deeply, deeply relaxed

Quietly breathe… in… out

Your eyelids are beginning to feel very, very heavy and tired

You will probably want to blink in a moment

When you start to blink, you can continue blinking

Just let things happen naturally now

Don't try too hard to make things happen

Don't try to stop things happening

Just let things fall into place

In a moment, your blinks will become slower... and bigger

Your eyes are becoming more and more tired

Your eyelids are becoming heavier and heavier

They are so heavy now... they want to close

When you feel you want to close them, let them close

Just let them close on their own

They want to close now, let them go, closing tighter

And tighter... tighter and tighter

Go to sleep

Sleep very, very deeply

Completely relax... give yourself up completely to this very relaxing...

pleasant drowsy feeling

Stop counting, now

Just sleep... sleep... sleep... very deeply

Sleep very, very deeply".

Deepening the Progressive Relaxation

"A feeling of relaxation is completely overcoming you, extending over your entire body

The muscles of your feet and ankles are relaxing completely

Let them go… completely limp and loose

Let them relax

The muscles of your thighs are relaxing completely

Let them relax… go completely limp and loose

As the muscles of your thighs and legs become completely relaxed and limp and loose, you are aware of a feeling of heaviness in your lower limbs

Your limbs now feel as though they are becoming as heavy as lead

Let your thighs and legs go

Let them feel as heavy as lead

Let them be completely relaxed

As they become relaxed, your sleep is becoming deeper, and deeper

The feeling of relaxation is now spreading upwards… over your entire body

Your stomach muscles are relaxing.. you're letting them go… limp and loose

Now your chest muscles are relaxing

Your back muscles feel limp and loose

You're letting them go limp and loose.. allowing them to relax

As this is happening, your whole body is becoming as heavy as lead

You want to sink down… deeper and deeper… into the chair

Let your body go... heavy as lead

Let it relax comfortably back... deeper and deeper... into the chair

As it does so, you are drifting deeper, slowly, deeper, pleasantly into a deeper and deeper sleep

Give yourself up completely... to this relaxed, drowsy, comfortable, pleasant, enjoyable feeling

Now this feeling of complete relaxation is spreading into the muscles of your arms... your shoulders... into your neck

Let your arm muscles relax

Let them relax... let them go... limp and loose

Let them relax

Your neck muscles, your facial muscles... they are quite relaxed... your eyes are closed... your eyelids relaxed completely

The muscles of your forehead...

To the crown of your head...

All completely relaxed...

Let your entire body go... let it be completely relaxed

Let it go limp and slack

As you do, your sleep is becoming deeper... deeper... deeper

As this feeling of complete relaxation is spreading and deepening right over and through your body you are falling into a very, very deep sleep

You are so deeply asleep, everything you now tell yourself to happen, will happen

Every feeling you say will experience... you will experience

Now, you must sleep... sleep very, very deeply

Deeper and deeper asleep... deeper and deeper asleep

Now, you are looking into the mirror…

The mirror is cloudy at first…

But the mist is clearing and now you can see an image

You're now going to look deeper into the mirror and describe what you see…

What do you see and what do you feel?

You're going to describe it…"

Wake Up Technique

Record this after the initial relaxation technique, on the same tape.
Repeat the following firmly and brightly, but quietly:

"In a few moments you will wake up by counting up to ten…

From one to ten…

Slowly, rhythmically…

Ten…

Nine… you are going to start to wake up

Eight… you feel more alert

Seven… you're coming round

Six… preparing to come back into the room

Five… you feel more awake

Four… breathing more shallowly now

Three… you're going to wake up in a moment

Two… your eyes are opening now

One… open your eyes

You're back in the room

You're awake

Feeling bright, alert, wide awake and wonderful"

Speak the final words more loudly with a bright and happy tone, almost
singing them.

The Language Of Reincarnation

Dharma and Karma

In all my research I have found no evidence of dharma and karma; that is, cause and effect. Being a bad person in a previous life does not directly mean suffering in this life.

However, if we accept that each life gives us experiences from which we can learn, then we can accept that we are working towards a 'whole', a 'perfect soul', and gaining what Eastern philosophy calls Nirvana.

Each significant experience in our lives is an opportunity to learn and thereby enrich our spirituality, even (in fact, particularly) the bad ones. If we do not do so and gain insight, it is quite common for the experience to be repeated, either during the same lifetime, or in another life. This can sometimes be very difficult when we are in the midst of a crisis or experiencing a drama or terrible calamity, but if we are able to reflect on this later, we may realise that something valuable has actually been learned.

The Chronology of Reincarnation

We tend to understand time as a linear process, but some theorists believe this is not the case, and that time can be represented as a wheel or circle, so that past lives accessed need not have happened in chronological order. In addition, when accessing past lives we might on occasion actually experience future lives, which can be rather confusing - but that is another debate to be examined in a future book.

Soul Mates

'Soul mates' are frequently referred to and discussed in everyday life. Sometimes the term is interpreted with a romantic slant, but this is not necessarily the case. I believe the soul is not one entity that moves as a whole from one being to another, but that it can split into a multitude of soul-pieces that then become part of a new being.

I believe this is the explanation for meeting soul mates, in other words, two beings containing part of the same soul 'recognise' each other. I believe it is also the origin of the phenomenon of many souls being reincarnated together, as in the case of the Albigensians. Thus the bond is not always directly romantic.

The Role of Dreams in Past Lives

The role of dream interpretation can provide a clue to past lives. This is usually the case when experiencing recurring dreams. However, it must be noted that recurring dreams can also be the subconscious mind's way of helping us to solve problems, and may not be directly linked to past lives.

Notwithstanding this, a recurring dream happening at a time when we are stressed may be a far memory (far memory is sometimes the spontaneous remembrance of something from a past life) of a trauma in that previous life, for example the point of death, or moments of danger in that particular past life. This can manifest itself in dreams where one is being chased, falling, or flying. So it is possible that we all have small glimpses of past lives through our dreams.

What is the point?

Understanding a lesson from a past life may be crystal clear, and you may have a revelation about yourself. Unfortunately, it is more likely that you will not fully understand the message.

Occasionally there may be a physical sign like a birthmark, mole or some other blemish on the body connecting an event in a past life to your present incarnation. An example of this came to light when I was conducting a past life regression with a country and western singer, who was surprised to find that in a past life she was a medieval man-at-arms and had died by an arrow in the back. Today she has a ten-inch-long, red birthmark just below her left shoulder blade.

There is no guarantee that a direct or symbolic implication will be achieved, and you may not fully understand the meaning of your regression. However, an attempt to interpret the experiences of your past life is always worthwhile.

Part Two

Peter's Story

Roman Ruins

I had listened intently to Peter as he recounted his experience. He was a white haired, 60-something farmer. His fenland, weathered face was tanned to a red glow; his eyes were closed and his brow knotted in thought. As his eyes opened the tears rolled.

It seemed to me his silent crying stung not only his rubicund face but all of his being. His large hands reached out in an open, honest prayer for forgiveness. The toil of years ingrained into his palm print added to his sense of guilt. I was at a loss to comprehend the intense emotions as he awoke from his trance, his altered state of awareness.

After a few moments had passed, Peter looked at me through moist and yet acutely aware, light green eyes.

"Sorry, sorry," he repeated. "But I've only told you half of it."

"There's more?" I enquired, almost incredulously.

"Oh yes," he murmured. Before I could reply he continued, "Oh yes indeed. When we started, I struggled focusing on seeing things." Scratching his forearm, then adjusting his rolled shirt sleeves, he began. "I was there, I could see people around me, hear them, smell things, touch things. I was warm, no hot. I fell to my knees."

Peter stopped for a breath, slowly stroking his tongue over his upper lips, as if tasting something. I was not prepared for what followed.

" She's beautiful," he murmured. "A beautiful woman," he added more clearly. "No more a child, such an angel of a face, I seemed lost in her stare, then I looked to her hands." At this, Peter stopped, looked heavenward, then closed his eyes. He seemed to smile; or was it a grimace? I could not interpret his heavily emotion-filled expression.

"Red, blood red were her hands. And the sound, a clatter." Without a pause for air he continued, "I knew, I knew everything, it was all there in my head, I know it all."

"Know what?" I urged with intrigue.

"My life," he stated.

"Your life?" I looked at him.

"No …yes," he seemed confused.

"You mean the past life?" I carefully suggested.

"That's it, me, him, the person I was."

He exhaled heavily.

"Do you want to continue?" I urged, feeling concerned. After a silence, broken by a choked sniffle from Peter, he continued.

"Yes, she was the last thing I saw, covered in blood, my blood. Then it all seemed to cloud over, just like a purple cloud. Then the clatter, I knew what that was. It was the sword. I had pulled it out of me. Before I lay in my own blood, I heard it hit the floor. I can still hear it …"

He shuddered.

It began to dawn on me just what was happening. Peter had arrived exactly at the point of death in a previous incarnation. What I was hearing was the end of a life, a violent and bloody end to a life. It was fascinating, just like the proverbial drowning man whose life passed before his eyes. This twentieth century man had become privy to another's life. My curiosity aroused, I wondered whether all the details were there, crystal clear, or perhaps fragmented, shattered into little pieces.

Peter's intense trance broke, his altered state was ended, but he had specifically said he knew everything.

"How are you feeling?" I enquired.

"Okay," he sighed heavily.

"Do you want to carry on?" I checked, still with concern.

"Yeah, yes I do," Peter assured me.

"In your own time, tell me as much as you can, as clearly as you can," I encouraged him.

After a gulp of water, Peter shared his revelations.

"I was in Rome, no what I mean is, I was from Rome," he continued.

"I did not see it all, I just remembered. She killed me, but with just cause. You see it was a great wrong I'd done her, and her family."

He spoke the words in an almost flat monotone, somewhat detached. As he spoke further, the whole story became clear.

Peter had been a man named Bucco. He was the eldest son of a southern Italian merchant, who had travelled the empire as a young man. He was a shrewd and competent trader, who had built the family wealth, so much so that moving in circles of the ruling classes was easy and natural. Before his thirtieth birthday, Bucco had bought a grand villa in the countryside, some short way from Rome.

Bucco's real downfall had begun in Sicily. He had acquired a sulphur mine with a money lender, Luc, of Messina, and Titus, a Roman legislator. Their acquisition was all above board, although not particularly ethical.

Bucco, a married man with two children, had begun to spend less and less time in his villa home, preferring the delights offered at Luc's palatial home. Though he kept an eye and a firm hand on business, he had become intoxicated by the hedonistic pleasures offered to him. His particular indulgence was a raven haired beauty, similar to him in age, with startlingly fair skin. Through all his philandering and appalling depravities, he always returned to this specific mistress. She was special, captivating and even he could not explain why he treated only her with respect. He lay with her most nights, sleeping off his drunken states. Rarely did he even attempt to embrace this beauty, almost as if he felt unworthy of her.

This enticing servant of Luc's villa, who had been brought south from the mountains of the Danube region in her childhood, knew little of her birth-land or kin. All she knew was her life in service of her master. However, she was a truly mysterious presence. Despite the sweltering Mediterranean sun, her skin remained fair, soft and unblemished. Her eyes were an intense dark brown, they seemed like black pools. Her voice was strangely captivating; when she spoke all listened. A daughter of Hades, Luc had called her, though he admitted she gave him no call for complaint, being exemplary in her duties, Despite the girl's outstanding beauty, it seemed that no one had ever taken her to any of the many feasts and nights of love games in the villa, that was until Bucco discovered her.

Their first coitus embrace had lacked passion and love, but from that night he had belonged entirely to her. To the outside world he appeared the master, she the slave; in reality the contrary was true. Yes, he continued his life of indulgence and self gratification; but when alone with her he acted with caution. His behaviour in her company was always polite and reserved, almost to the point of obedience.

The romantic spell was eventually broken when he returned from a long and demanding time spent in Rome. The night he arrived at the straits of Messina, a great storm blackened the sky. Dramatic hail, thunder and lightning of all colours seemed to scar the sky. A great downpour left him and his party drenched at the quayside. Miserable, cold and unprotected they weathered the angry night.

The grey, glum morning was nevertheless welcome. A calm sea meant an early departure to Sicily was possible and welcome. It was late afternoon of the next day before they reached Luc's villa. Though there had been no repeat of the storm, the sky remained murky and dark, with no sun breaking through. Glints of red, orange and yellow occasionally flashed through the clouds. Although Luc's residence was very much a working villa, almost a town in itself, Bucco was overwhelmed by the hectic energy in the place; he had never seen so much activity.

Even though it was too early to bathe as the furnace had not yet heated the waters to the desired temperature, Bucco divested after using the communal latrines and plunged into the luke warm water. He stayed in the bath until his skin pruned and reddened as the water eventually heated up. That night he slept deeply. But when he woke he felt disturbed. He was not able to remember his dreams, but he was certain that demons of the night had infested his mind. From his own quarters he could see across to Luc's private yard. Everyone was taking breakfast, so he banished his disturbed thoughts from his mind and joined them, exchanging brief greetings as he took his seat. Bucco refused food, but gladly drained a goblet of pomegranate cordial and watered wine. The sky remained dull and overcast, and most of the talk was of the weather and the havoc wreaked in the vineyards. The common consensus was that the gods were unhappy, why else should the sun have vanished? As talks furthered, the blame was beginning to be pointed at Valamessina, the dark eyed, fair skinned temptress of Bucco.

Luc put his arm around his friend, and led him into the courtyard, pointing to the old Greek temple, which crowned the flat topped mountain that had dominated the vista for what seemed like always. As those dear friends stood together, things became clearer; settled again after his absence, the events of recent days came to Bucco. It seemed that Valamessina had given birth to a girl on exactly the same night that the dreadful storm had begun. There were wild rumours that she had made a pact with the underworld gods, in rejection of the Roman ones, as well as performing rituals of blood sacrifices and rites of Hades. Apparently also, a free man, who was her kin, had visited the premises and paid for her freedom. It seemed that now they were gone, much to the relief of the household.

So much had happened in such a short time, that Bucco could hardly comprehend all of the extreme revelations. However, more followed. On leaving, Valamessina had abandoned the child, where exactly though no one knew. It later transpired that the distressed mother had left her daughter at the steps of the old Greek temple. The abandoned infant, just hours old, was discovered by the grace of Venus, heard wailing by young lovers at their tryst. Luc explained to Bucco that the vulnerable child was safe, suckling with a nurse of Luc's house. He took great care to explain all of the details to his friend, because, he ventured, surely this child was also Bucco's daughter.

Intensely affected by the news, Bucco was detached from everyone for the following few days. Without acknowledging the child, he left for Rome. There, he visited his friend and advisor Titus, who, after some persuasion bought Bucco's share of the mine, in effect letting him wash his hands completely of Sicily.

Titus and his wife, Petula, were childless, and as well as the taking of the extra share in the mine, he also took on the orphan, who became their child with all the privileges of a good Roman family.

As time passed, Bucco's and Titus' families grew together, almost as cousins. A great friendship grew between Marcus and Alanius, the sons of Bucco, and Melissina, Titus' adopted child, without her ever knowing of her true roots.

Eighteen summers had passed since Bucco had left Sicily for the last time. The years had only soured his heart like a spoilt wine. Not a day had passed without memories of Valamessina invading his thoughts. On the surface he played his role, but inside he was emotionally dry and hollow.

It was a balmy, sunny day when Titus brought news of a soothsayer at Caesar's court, who for the world had everything of Valamessina about her. At first Bucco thought Titus spoke of this simply to enlighten him and no more. But it was actually the man's own fear for his child, the daughter he had come to love so much. He wanted Bucco, as a true friend, to ensure Melissina was safe from any claim or spoiling from this dark woman from their past.

Bucco was surprised at his own senses. A flood of emotions raged through his entire body on hearing the mention of Valamessina. But over the years he had become an expert in disguising his true feelings. If any glimmer of upset had shown in his eyes, he was sure Titus saw none of it. Titus wanted him to help rid them of the threat from the woman; .Bucco abruptly resisted any involvement. He tried to detach himself from his friend's problem, emphasising the empty insistence that the dark woman had no power. After all, she could only be an oracle at best; a charlatan at worst, surely she could be no harm, he feebly reassured his friend. How wrong he had been!

On the night of the full moon, Titus was found hanging from a laburnum tree by his left leg. His wrist had been slashed and his mouth was stuffed with the yellow flowers of the laburnum, barely a drop of blood left in his lifeless body. The investigations that ensued threw up many possible explanations and suspects, but the tangled web surrounding Titus' death proved to be unsolvable.

Bucco knew exactly who was responsible, when he received a gift of pomegranates from an anonymous sender. The bizarre gift had been grotesquely impregnated with blood, obviously that of his friend. However, Bucco did not interpret the parcel as a threat to himself; he saw it as a severe warning only. Nevertheless, he felt concern for Petula, his friend's now vulnerable widow.

Whether Bucco's motives were for protection or revenge he did not know, but he set out on a route of no return. He enlisted the help of a senator who had several bully boys skilled in disposing, conveniently, of anyone who was deemed a threat to a paying customer. Bucco parted with his gold and waited for the news of Valamessina's demise. It never came. Instead, she contacted Bucco, inviting him to her rooms at Ceasar's palace. Once there, in her powerful presence he saw how futile any attack on this powerful woman seemed. Nonetheless his fear drove him to find some way, to somehow dispatch this black-hearted woman, before Petula met her end and Melissina came under Valamessina's spell. His despair grew when she quietly handed him back his own gold. She whispered to him the news of how the intended assassins had met their end. Valamessina carefully explained to him that she was well protected, with great friends and power.

It took many months before Bucco's chance arose. Valamessina had wanted him close, and encouraged regular visits from him. Despite her guile, she saw Bucco as ineffectual and impotent towards her, with no courage himself.

Valamessina felt no pain, only surprise, incredible surprise when the sword in Bucco's hand sliced through her throat. She dropped to the stone floor. Her eyes were fixed open, still watching him in astonished disbelief that this weak man who had never got blood on his own hands would dare to attack her in such an intimate and daring way.

Bucco did not worry about any consequences. The political climate was changing, the balance of power shifting to make new alliances that had given him confidence in the new senate. Also, he felt complete relief because now that Valamessina was dead, her menacing henchmen would also vanish.

After cleaning himself in a daze, and having all traces of the murderous deed removed, he made his way to see Petula and set her mind at rest. Unfortunately, his arrival was too late, Petula was already dead, by whose hand it was not known. But Bucco felt certain that it must be the work of Valamessina, even in death she could still reach out her hand to touch and mortally slay. As for Melissina, she was safe with Alanius, Bucco's youngest son, unaware of the tragedy in her own house. However, Bucco was aware that looming over him was the truth, the awful and inevitable telling of the secrets of his past, and the full truth of who Melissina really was.

The months slowly passed. The time never seemed appropriate, so Bucco avoided facing the inevitable. Again he chose the easy option, to let the wolf sleep, and do no harm. Melissina had settled and become quite happy considering the gruesome misfortunes surrounding her. She resided in a new, secure family environment, with Marcus and Alanius giving her every possible attention, these cousins in friendship were close as any siblings.

Bucco felt pleased that the girl seemed so contented. Financially comfortable, Melissina's inheritance made her even more attractive to the most eligible of Roman suitors, and marrying her into a good family would present no difficulty. However, the gods chose to interfere further.

Just when all seemed settled, Alanius announced his intentions of marrying Melissina, proclaiming to Bucco his undying love for the girl. This was no youthful infatuation, he insisted, but a deep and real love, grown over the years of closeness, now burning bright. The colour drained from Bucco's face as he heard the words. His whole being crumpled as though Neptune clutched at his soul and was pulling him beneath the seas; he was drowning inside. Without a thought to the panicked words he uttered, with loud anger he absolutely forbade any such union. Grasping Alanius roughly by the arm, he forcefully led the young man away, still ranting his objection before all who witnessed the unreasonable outburst. Onlookers were bemused, considering it incredible that he should find such aggressive fault in what, for all purposes, was an appropriate and happy match.

Within a few days, Alanius was pressed into his father's business in the Aegean isles, to keep him out of harm's way and cool hi heart with taxing work.

Melissina was a different problem,not so easily exiled, she was as much a guest in her new abode, a member of the family in everyone's eyes, so needed the respect as such. Stealing himself with as much strength as he could muster, Bucco prepared himself to finally confess all to his oblivious daughter; the truth would out. Almost contritely he invited her to join him for a walk through the vineyard to the hill top, a wonderfully peaceful place to sit, think and watch the world. Occasionally he had sat there in solitude, or to ask favour of the gods. Hardly knowing where to begin, he stumbled through the whole complicated story of how she had come into the world. He described the abandonment and subsequent adoption into Titus and Petula's lives, as well as the death of her natural mother by his hand. He attempted to also explain his part in rejecting her, describing how when she had found a good and happy life he had felt no guilt over her. He explained his new concern over the attempted love match, reasoning that he had never perceived any thought of love between the children, other than that of siblings.

He justified to the girl that, on hearing Alanius declare his feeling of love between man and woman, he no other option but to intervene and prevent things going any further. Meissina and Alanius were young, he explained. There would be plenty of chances for other love, other people, and what seemed so intense now would shortly pass, this passion would fade, he insisted.

When he had finished all he had to say, he braced himself for the inevitable torrent. However, Melissina did not respond. In silence, she just remained seated, hugging her legs to her body and resting her chin on her knees, staring transfixed on some unseen thing. There was no word, no scream of anger, no objection to this impossible revelation, nothing.

Bucco waited, caught in the trance of the distant, lost stare in Melissina's eyes. The day moved into twilight and the evening breeze broke her reverie. Without any warning, she suddenly jumped up and ran. Bucco did not move, he remained seated and followed with his eyes in her wake. The moments slipped on; after the sun had sunk below the west completely, he slowly pulled himself up and made his gradual way home, uncertain of what to expect now that all was laid open.

Bucco was the master of his own house, but as he entered his home he felt uncomfortable and anxious. It did not take him long to recover his authority. The sound of cracking pots and an orgy of screams coming from the east wing angered him. Bucco followed the din, only to find Melissina raging in the kitchen, as his family and household staff stood by, watching this angry whirlwind of destruction. When all but a few things were broken, the girl collapsed and wept inconsolably. Bucco bellowed at the onlookers, ordering everyone out. His wife, Cornelia, just stood still with confused pain etched upon her face, watching the scene sadly, without uttering a word. Marcus went to Melissina and gently urged her to her feet, guiding the tearful girl to her chamber.

More revelations followed, as that night Cornelia discovered every single detail about Melissina. Cornelia's heavy heart was saddened by Melissina's painful circumstances. The girl's life had been completely messed up: her love now forbidden because of blood ties. Cornelia, with no concern for her own distress at the truth of her husband's antics, attempted to comfort the inconsolable Melissina. She carefully murmured to the girl that at least the relationship was better to end now, before a marriage and offspring spoilt by such a union of blood. No words even came close to soothing the poor girl's devastated heart. Melissina withdrew into herself, rejecting any compassion offered.

More than a week had passed when Melissina came to find Bucco, who was alone and working in his study. He was relieved to see that she seemed bright, full of colour with a real flush to her cheeks. Yet he had severely misread her glowing look, she was not back in health but in fact approached him with a smouldering anger. She fingered the Iberian blade positioned proudly in the room, slowly and precisely lifting it from its sheath; she knew this was the sword that had taken the life of the mother she had never known. She gently cradled the sword to her breast, almost nursing it as a mother would a child. With a sinister vagueness she began to tell what exactly had passed between her and Alanius. Bucco's hopes were about to be shattered, any hope of some good to come was destroyed.

Melissina told of how she and Alanius were already lovers, how much happiness they had enjoyed in each others arms, and how they had lain together. Worse still, the damage was already done, she was some months with child. Bucco was astounded by the details. He moved closer to her, but she stepped back, aggressively rejecting any such attempt. Bucco's eyes closed and if he could have closed his ears he would have, he did not want to hear her voice or see her face as the damaging words came out. After a weighted pause, she then coldly and deliberately informed her father that she had taken a Jupiter berry.

Bucco's mind fell into a whirl. He panicked, wondering how she could possibly have come by such a thing. Only a few people knew of the Jupiter berry, a hard skinned, pea-like fruit used in trials of ordeal and the priests of the temples in rites of truth. If swallowed whole, its hard skin would stay intact, unaffected by the digestion of the stomach, but if chewed, its poison would be released and would kill, slowly and painfully. To have the man she loved denied her, and to be expecting an abomination; to live was not bearable, and as he opened his eyes he now saw the apparently healthy red glow was not what it had seemed, but was in reality the onset of death from the deadly bite of the Jupiter berry. At that same moment, he saw the blood on her clothes and hands. In his understanding of what was happening, the pain from the sword he now pulled from his body ripped his liver wide open. The sword fell from his hand to the floor. She had plunged the blade deep into his stomach as her final act before her own life gave up.

Peter looked into his hands, lost in thought. Sensing the intensity of the recollection he had disclosed, I decided to wait a while before speaking.

"Peter," I said, after some time. There was no reply."Peter," I spoke his name again, but he just sat gazing into his hands.

Then without warning he lifted himself to his feet, and walked to the window. Looking out he began, "It's a lovely day."

"Yes," I agreed.

"I'm glad I was born here," he continued. "I've had a hard life and sometimes a lonely one." He turned to face me, speaking softly."Nonetheless I'm glad because until I was born I was in limbo."

I remained silent, not quite sure where he was going with what he was saying.

"When it all cleared…" he continued.

"What cleared?" I encouraged.

"The fog, I was in a kind of mist, it was warm and light. At first it was like a dark purple swirl, and then it was a lilac mist. It cleared, and I was outside, outside of me. But I could see everything and I knew everything."

He made his way back over to me and sat down again. Looking at me, his eyes began to fill.

"I could see my lifeless body turning the marble floor crimson, then Melissina fell to her knees and with clenched hands she beat my body. The she swooned to her own death.,"

Peter spoke clearly, without the tremble in his voice. Wiping his eyes he started again.

"Then I was rolling and tumbling, but slowly without any worry. I could not see how or why I was moving. When I stopped I was alone in a field of the greenest grass, broken here and there by red poppies, indigo irises and yellow daisies. The sky was a beautiful azure, with occasional silver edged clouds, hiding a sun that was sending magical rays from heaven to earth. I began to walk,but I met no one. So I just walked and walked. Still I met no one. I waited for night, but it did not come. I walked on and on, it seemed many hours had passed, if not days.

Nothing changed, the sky was the same, the flowers in the field, though I must surely have walked many miles, nothing moved. I did not reach the irises or the poppies ever as I walked towards them. The sun stayed behind the same rich azure. I stopped walking and just stood, watching and waiting. No hunger or thirst did I feel, nor did I need sleep, there was no pain or feeling of any kind. No laughter, no joy, no satisfaction; just existing, waiting and waiting…" Peter paused, before scratching his head with both hands. He looked at me , "That was my limbo, you see, two thousand years, lost, wasted."

I wanted to say something to the man, but there were no words remotely appropriate. He eventually broke the awkward moment.

"Suddenly someone spoke to me," Peter began to smile as he told me the rest of his experience.

"I turned to see who was talking, and there beside me was a young man, he seemed familiar.

'May I sit with you?' he asked.

I opened my mouth to reply, but no words came.

'May I?' he repeated, as he sat next to me.

I adjusted my position so I was sitting opposite him, looking into his eyes.

'It is high time you left here.'

He spoke the words softly and clearly.

Many questions, such as How? Who? What was going on? ran through my brain. I wanted to know where he came from , after so many years of solitude, Why now? Who was he?

'Who I am is not the question.' He said. He smiled easily at me on seeing my obvious puzzlement.

'What?' I blurted out, the sound of my own voice surprised me.

'Who are you? is the question,' he answered.

And do you know, I could not answer, I really did not know.

'I don't know,' I said eventually.

'Oh,' he said. 'That's a pity.'

'What?' I exclaimed, shaking my head in anger at this enigmatic stranger.

'Be calm, all will be clear.' Standing up he then offered his hand to me and said 'Come, come with me.'

I took his hand , it felt good, strong and comforting. Once to my feet, I seemed his equal - the same height and build - it occurred to me I could be looking at myself. Except , he was not me. He knew where he was going, and I had no idea. We walked shoulder to shoulder, though I kept just a little behind, so as to follow his lead.

'Do you remember anything?' he then enquired.

'No,' I answered.

As I replied,I realised night had fallen. I can't remember when I last saw the stars, and seeing them took my breath away. Not a cloud, a beautiful night of endless stars, which shone brilliantly.

'You must go alone now,' he said, directing me towards the sea. Without me ever noticing, we had reached a sea shore, we stood on the beach, the waves beginning to lap at my feet. In that moment I felt afraid, but also drawn to go deeper into the sea.

Soon the water covered my middle, I then realised I was naked. I turned back to the shore to look for my companion, but he was gone. Then a wave covered me, so I began to swim, and as my confidence grew I dived below the waves to swim under the sea. I was not breathless - I could swim without weariness. I felt warm, happy, at peace. After some time I realised others were swimming, many people and creatures of the sea. Then I saw a light. I was inexorably pulled towards the light.. As I got closer, all the memories flooded back. Suddenly I was choking and coughing, gasping for breath, and surrounded by light. I was reborn."

On finishing his fantastic and vivid description, Peter smiled a wide, contented grin.

"I'm glad to be alive," he said. "But I know this time I have lived a good life, and I'm not afraid of death."

Barbara's Story

Redcoat Recollection.

Barbara, a complete paranormal sceptic, had volunteered with two friends to be subjects in a Paranormal television programme being filmed at Frazer Castle, near Aberdeen. Barbara, Monica and Sandra were the first amongst the audience to raise their hands, and be duly brought by an assistant producer to me for rehearsal. I was waiting in a medieval dining room, furnished with antiques from several periods since the initial building of this cold, highland fortress. As I looked around, the wood - panelled room looked odd, full of monitors, technicians and the veritable army that is needed to make a modern day television programme.

I had managed to annex a corner of the room with several large comfortable chairs of varying styles. Portable heaters had also been brought in, against the castle's natural ability to maintain the cold.

After the initial introductions, the three ladies made themselves comfortable in the luxurious chairs. It only took a few moments to establish that both Monica and Sandra were most eager and interested to experience a past life regression; however, Barbara was visibly less keen. Her nervousness was masked by fits of giggles, but not to be the odd one out, she began to relax and joined in the spirit of the session.

I used a method of progressive relaxation, which in terms of technique is similar to hypnosis, allowing the subject to reach a state of altered awareness. This state of awareness can be described as an almost trance-like state; although the conscious mind is completely aware of what is happening, at the same time the subconscious is able to express itself. This state allows us to access the subconscious directly, which is not possible in the normal state of awareness.

Some thirty minutes had passed before any reaction occurred. Monica could only see cloud in her visualised mirror, and there was not much more to report for Sandra, as she saw a reflection so unclear that it just faded into a mist.

I was about to abandon the session, as I had no thought that Barbara would be able to experience any form of regression either. Clicking my fingers to break the trance, Monica and Sandra blinked their eyes open, but Barbara suddenly bellowed: "Away you brute!" before opening her eyes. We all looked at her, as the rest of the room also fell silent, now focusing on my little group.

Dismissing the captivated attention of the rest of the room, I again turned to my subjects. As a trio they were confident, but I knew that if I separated Barbara from the others, she would probably lose her courage. So I kept them together for the session.

Over the next hour Barbara recounted an extraordinary past life. I was concerned that, as she returned to the normal state of awareness, she may not return to that particular past life; it would be a great pity not to record what seemed to be such an eventful life. Rehearsals drew to a close and it was then time to film in front of an audience in the main hall of the castle. The cameras. Rolling to capture the events of that day, got perhaps more than was expected or even hoped for.

The face of the mercurial presenter was a picture to behold, as Barbara, entranced after further progressive relaxation, began to speak.

"It's cold," she complained, hugging herself.

"Where are you?" I asked.

Even with her eyes closed it was evident that she was puzzled by my voice, it did not belong to the place she now was. Despite her apparent confusion, she continued with an outburst.

"Yeh bastard!" she suddenly shouted.

"Who, who is?" I asked, very gently.

She screwed her face up and shook her head.

"Ah whisht, can ye no see the great ugly brut?" she spat.

Placing my hand on her forehead, I spoke to her quietly.

"Relax," I soothed. "Relax," I again urged, trying to calm her down.

I spent a few months establishing a rapport with her, thus enabling her to accept and become comfortable with my disembodied voice.

"Tell me your name?" I asked.

With her eyes closed and with no expression on her face, she announced: "Mary O'Carroll".

This surprised me, as most people when recounting a past life usually struggle with names and more often than not only the given name is used.

"Mary, may I call you Mary?" I enquired firmly.

"Yes" she replied, softly but clearly.

"Tell me all you see and what is happening."

From then on she told everything without inference from me. Her account is recalled here just as she told it:

"I was standing in the snow and it was still snowing. We were all there, cold, afraid, angry and crying. We were shouting and screaming at him. He sat on his horse, just strutting up and down in front of us, smirking.

I had the measure of him, a murdering bastard, with a heart of stone. Arrogant, astride his white steed in his red coat, he ordered his men to remove us. There were ten of them, all thugs. The King's shilling and their soiled red coats gave them the authority to brutally push us back. I fell from the blow of a rifle, but it was not the force as much as the shock that sent me sprawling. Once finding my feet again the small, red line had moved beyond me. Scattering some forty odd women and children, that's all we were. Looking back to see the beast of a man, his cruel face obviously enjoyed the violent scene he had inflicted. He paid me no attention as he dismounted and climbed the five steps leading to the church door.

The church was the reason we had all come. It was the only building of any size in the village. The cold was beginning to bite, and for the first time that day I grew worried for my children. The snow became heavier, and in the panic I began to shout their names. Thankfully they were at my side in no time. We women found ourselves again, and after some talk we came to the conclusion, out of urgency, to make our way to Clairy's farm. Unlike us they had been left untouched . A barn at the farm was ample enough to house our urgent need.

As night fell, exhaustion and weariness overcame me, and with my three daughters cuddled into me, I succumbed to sleep. It was still night when I awoke. Easing myself free of my daughters I made my way through the numerous slumped sleeping bodies to the barn door. Gently easing the latch I peered out. The chill outside stung my face and turned my breath to white smoke against the night.

The snow had been heavy, coating everything, so much so that the previous day's awful events were hidden. The moon, waxing to the full,illuminated the snow and gave me the eyes of a cat seeing in the night.

From my position I had a good view of Clairy's yard and house, but nothing moved, nothing to see but a white covering. Closing the latch port, I soon felt the heaving warmth of the overpopulated barn. Once bedded down again with my children, I hoped for sleep; instead my head was full of the morning before, when Hell came to earth. Tom, my husband, was always up and about before me, but when I awoke yesterday morn he was still deep in his sleep. A smell of something scorching broke my sleep, and I roused Tom in a panic that our home may be burning. We quickly found our house safe, but the burning smell was strong. Once outside there was little to see at first, just a dark night with snow lying in a small flurry. Suddenly a hue and cry went up from our closest neighbour, so we ran towards the Jacksons'. On reaching the top of the brow, all was plain. The small village was burning and several outlying crofts were also alight. The hungry flames were no accident, but some grave deed of intent.

In urgency we returned back to our home and roused the children. Tom and my son Dominic dressed and booted against the cold weather, and then left us to see what help they could give. As they left without a kiss or embrace, Tom shouted that I should leave with the lasses and go to the church. Without breaking the night, quickly we left for the church. Taking only half a loaf and some cheese, I mounted Patricia and Connie on Lingo, our only horse, whilst my elder daughter, Megan, and I trudged along side. The snow was beginning to stick and the cold wind chilled the lasses, but we kept hope knowing we would soon the church and sanctuary. There were others, out at this early hour, all of us heading in the same direction. The smell of smoke now became more acrid, as the full reason for the fire became harrowingly clear.

A platoon of redcoats, some bearing flaming torches, led by a mounted captain, was sweeping the countryside. They were in front of us from the right, making their way to the village. I stopped in my tracks as I saw several soldiers run ahead of their fellows, and scorch Fergill's smithy and home. I was planted where I stood, unable to move forward or back, as I stood there quite frozen, in fear as well as cold. Without noticing at first, I was joined by others, all in the same state; all full of worries at what was happening and what it meant. The snow was getting thicker, and this was no place or time to stand and wonder. With renewed urgency and strength in camaraderie, we, some score in number, trudged on. Listening to the chatter around me, I realised we were women and children only, there were no men amongst us. I soon discovered from my neighbours how their men had been taken and their houses burnt. This really sent my head spinning and my stomach turning in sickness; I was glad no food had been taken that morn.

My worry was held in abeyance that Tom and Dominic were not taken, but had set off themselves to see what could be done. Surely they were safe and free, but doubt shadowed my mind; if the soldiers had them we would be none the wiser. All this and more worry ran around my head. Connie's cries that she was hungry stopped my mind's turmoil. So I halted awhile and broke bread for my daughters; I had no need for food now. By then we were at the rear of this pathetic procession to the church. Once there, we numbered some fairly miserable souls, but in all this despair I was joyed to find my sister, Anne, and her children. After tight hugs, I learnt her plight was worse than mine. Callum, my brother through marriage, had been dragged away, coshed and unconscious, and maybe even dead now, their croft razed to the ground as was many a home here about.

The main concern for now was to have shelter and maybe some peace inside God's house. This was not to be; it seemed the redcoats barred our entry, the church would be no refuge. The rumour amongst the women came to my ears, that this sacred place was now a prison for all our menfolk. Taken and imprisoned; but why? I could not comprehend, or know of any reason why this wreckage should befall our community. It was then that I was swept up in the screaming and shouting directed at that captain, that brute who had brought such misery and destruction on us.

Morning broke in the barn, with dust specs dancing in beams of sunlight against the early darkness inside the still shuttered barn. I could see dark shadows moving as mothers awoke, and quietly gathered themselves in uncertainty of what to do. In yesterday's confusion, no one had thought or felt the need to ask permission to lodge in the barn. The worries of yesterday were pushed aside as the needs of today called for action. I was, with my sister, urged by the rest to go and find out from Clairy what was about. This was no great hardship, as the Clairys were our good friends, as close as family.

We arrived at Jack Clairy's kitchen door and called for him; but no answer came back. I opened the door and we called again, but all was still. I made my way in, but Anne felt the better for staying at the doorway. Continuing to call out, I slowly made my way through the house, anxious at what I may find, but no one was home. It looked to me as though they were gone, and in a hurry too, but if they knew what was to happen why leave and tell no one, or give warning? Making my way back to the kitchen,

I called Anne in, and between us we looked for provisions. Thankfully both pantry and larder were still filled to the rafters; in readiness for winter. At least today we and all the others would eat well.

Not wanting to attract attention, we left both range and fire unlit, despite the cold. We returned to the barn with the welcome news of enough to eat for all. Anne took everyone back to the house, but I went to the loft, as from there I knew I would be able to have a good view of the church.

I could also view the surrounding countryside, which had become a white-out. Nothing stirred, and I wanted so much to glimpse Tom and Dominic, to be eased in my mind. After some time spent watching, with nothing about to happen, I felt hunger remind me that too long had passed since I last ate. Carefully leaving the loft, I made my way to the farmhouse. Once inside, the scene that met me sickened my heart. Lots of children were about, content enough with bellies full, but the women had faces telling a story of no joy, only the sheer pain of missing partners. The heartache in that room was so tangible I felt it with every breath. In the cold light of day all conversation had been stolen away, replaced only by pensive silence. After devouring a goodly portion of cured shank and fortifying myself with a pot of ale, I was ready to return to the church.

Somehow, by the time I had finished breakfast the women had found their strength. I suppose in any crisis that spirit just comes along in talk. Bernadette Jackson and I left the others at Clairy's and set off to the church. It seemed wise to go discreetly, and find what we could. The two of us, though afraid of what might greet us, felt the need to know what this business was all about.

When we came to the church all was quiet, and the night's snowfall had hidden what had passed yesterday. Together we entered, easing the heavy oak door open. Inside, the heat from half a dozen braziers made the church unusually warm. A number of bench pews had been arranged to make a pen, which housed the missing men. A dozen or more soldiers were in repose or sleeping; whilst another four casually guarded their prisoners.

As soon as we walked forward on the stone flagged floor the sound of our steps resounded to the rafters. Several heads turned our way, and one lean, unshaven red-coated man, bearing stripes on his sleeve, adjusted his crumpled uniform. He barked at us to go no further. At this the men held in the pen rose to their feet, but at sword and rifle point were ordered back down to sit on the floor. In that brief moment every face amongst the men was imprinted into my mind, but alas there was no Tom or Dominic. In an almost gentle tone this sergeant urged us to be gone before the Captain's expected return at midday.

I was insane with worry, so scared, not just for my own plight; I began to vent all my anger on this indifferent man, who wore the English King's coat. By the time I had exhausted all the curses known to me on these devils, Bernadette pulled me away and pushed me outside. Once in the cold I turned on her, still in anger. Shouting, she struck me hard with her back hand, right across the mouth. I was about to hit back; but she held me tightly and firmly explained to me through tears that when I was in the church, she had managed a few words with her husband.

Once back at Clairy's farm house we lit the fire and stove. Bernadette Jackson knew we were not to be bothered for now. She had learned from her husband that the soldiers were about to move once the weather eased, they were done here. Done with what? We all awaited to know, but she had no real answer, just something in the back of her memory. It could be a clearance, like way back, to her kinfolk in the highlands of Scotland.

This speculation was all well and good, but I needed to know why had happened to my husband and son. Taking an extra shawl I went back to the barn loft to look out for any sign of them. The sky was clear and blue, and even though it stayed bitterly cold, the sun shone brightly. This combined to make the white of the snow difficult to look out on. I was forced by the stark brightness to close my eyes or look away often. It seemed pointless, I was about to give up, but then something moved. Rubbing my eyes I focused through a narrow squint and was rewarded.

Among the subtle fold of the white blanket of snow that draped the countryside, I could just make out two figures appearing and disappearing in the undulating winter landscape.

There was no mistake, it was Tom and Dominic, free but in grave danger so close to the village. I needed to warn them of what I knew, so they could flee away and avoid capture.

I dashed back to the farmhouse and found a pair of Clairy's breeches to wear under my skirts to keep the brutal cold out. I mounted Lingo. Wearing men's pants and my sister's overcoat I was well muffled, as I rode out to find my men, setting off for the west of the village, in the direction I had last seen them. I must have made a conspicuous figure on a chestnut mare, standing out against the bright white open fields...."

At this stage of the account Barbara fell silent. After a few tense seconds I realised she was finished for now. Snapping my fingers in front of her face, she opened her eyes with quite a start.

"Barbara, Barbara can you hear me?" I asked.

She replied that yes she could hear me.

"Good. Can you remember what you were saying?" I prompted.

"Yes, I think so… but it was Ireland, not Scotland," she gushed. As she spoke her face held an expression of sheer puzzlement.

"How do you feel?" I checked.

"Great, I feel really good," she insisted, beaming. "I remember so much, it was though I was really there,I felt it all," she explained.

"You stopped suddenly, with a lot more to be seen. Do you know more, or why you stopped?" I encouraged her, curious to know more.

"No," she stated, but her tone was less than firm.

"Then I will end the session. However, there is a good chance over the next few days that more will come to you. You may even remember all of the life, that previous incarnation," I advised her.

I continued to talk to Barbara to remove the post hypnotic suggestion. We then spent several minutes discussing the events that had emerged during the session. Eventually the cameras stopped rolling.

We left the filming area and descended a stone spiral staircase, which led to the castle's kitchen. This spacious kitchen was obviously medieval, but thoughtful design had seen it fitted out with all the modern conveniences of today. In this cosy kitchen, dominated by a large table in the centre of the room, we sat and continued to discuss what had passed.

"I want to go back," Barbara announced to me, her eyes wide. I spent some time going over everything that had come through during the session. It seemed that events had just stopped suddenly, and I explained how that often happens in past life recall.

"There may be no more to find," I continued.

"No," she insisted. "I know why I stopped you see, as I was going through it I just thought I was in Scotland, but then I suddenly realised I was in Ireland. That confused me, it seemed to break what was going on, but I know there is more."

The room was bustling with film crew, castle staff and several psychics, all enjoying hot chocolate, tea, coffee and biscuits. It became obvious to others as the noise settled in the room that Barbara was about to return to her past life regression. Chairs were pulled up around the table and everyone hushed in eager anticipation.

I asked Barbara to make herself comfortable, be relaxed and to not concern herself with the others around the room. I then gently asked her to close her eyes and imagine she was back on the horse, back in the place she had been before. Once a person has experienced a hypnotic trance, it is possible to induce the same state by simply putting your thought precess in the same frame of mind. So by imagining the state, the trance can be recreated.

After a few moments, Barbara's breathing became deeper and her eyes, though closed fast, began to flicker in REM (Rapid Eye Movement, a sleep like state). I asked her to tell me what she could see. She then again began her recount as if there had been no break in its telling. She continued from the stage where she had been on horseback looking for her husband and son:

"I came to the area where I was sure I'd seen them, but alas there was no sight. I looked for footprints, and found none, so I moved on and then south behind the church to find a road that ran behind the churchyard and woodland. I then came across disturbed snow, it looked to me as though someone was trying to hide their tracks. My instinct was to follow the disturbed snow into the woods. I was about to dismount when it occurred to me that, if anyone saw me, and if Tom and Dominic were hiding in the wood, I could lead the redcoats to them. So I continued along the line of the wood, only hoping that if anyone should see me, it would be Tom.

I came to the edge of the wooded area, where the landscape opened to a vast, white covered valley. My disappointment at finding nothing was put aside, when a row of shouts came from the church. I retreated into the trees to watch this sudden activity. Now dismounted, I quietly guided my horse deep into cover and kept out of sight to espy all.

The men were marched out, flanked by redcoats on either side and led to the mounted captain; they set off across the valley. As they came closer to my position, I withdrew behind a large evergreen and held my breath in nervous fear. Suddenly, from behind me a rough hand came across my face, clasping my mouth and nose; another arm came around me and pulled me close to the assailant's body. My heart raced in panicked terror, as this strong individual yanked me back. Hot breath hit me as he quickly whispered for me to be silent and not to worry. Despite the fear and shock, my heart was eased as I recognised the voice. It was Jack Clairy, I nodded my head in acknowledgment as he released his grip.

I turned to face him, but before I spoke he put a finger to my lips and hushed me. Whether he knew my questions or not; he began to tell me, as he led me and my chestnut into a hollow clearing in the wood. The clearing was a warm, protected place, despite the day's cold. Jack told me how he had learned that a clearing of the land was about to happen. He had flitted away some days before with his family. He regretted telling no one, and was afraid to linger, but had come back to help give word. However, it was too late now, the harm was done, so he instead had kept out of sight, watching over what was happening.

Apparently, he explained to me, the rumour was that the men were being taken to Derry, then to be transported to Liverpool, and from there no one was certain. I wanted to know: What about us women and children? Clairy did not know; just that we were for clearing, to be shut off. I then excitedly told Jack that Tom and Dominic were not with the rest of the men, but free, and hereabout somewhere. Jack looked away from me, falling deadly silent, his reaction chilled me. I grabbed him and pulled his face towards mine; but his refusal to look into my eyes told of some deed that I feared to know.

I pleaded with him to tell me what had befallen them, but he just shook his head and pulled away. I would not let it go; he knew something, that was clear. In desperation I threatened to scream and alert the redcoats of our whereabouts, so he reluctantly told me what he had seen. Like me, he had seen them moving across the valley. He had been making his way to meet them, when he noticed redcoats also moving towards them. Jack told me how they had been taken into the church, but they had not been amongst the men marched out when the redcoats had left.

I was elated, they must be safe at the church, left unwanted. Why exactly, I did not know or think on , I just ran from the woods toward the church . Jack followed , leading Lingo, but I was racing as fast as I could in the deep snow. Shouting out for Tom and Dominic, I burst into the church.

The light from the only stained glass window above the altar, depicting a sacred heart image of Christ, set the church from my view into silhouette.

As my eyes grew accustomed to this enigmatic light, the shadows began to form into grisly clarity. Father Umber was grimly holding onto the legs of a heavy man. The priest was desperately pushing upward, trying in vain to ease the weight on the rope pulling around the neck of a man with a face distorted and bloodied in pain and death.

A new light was thrown onto the priest and hanging corpse, as Jack opened the church door. In that instant of illumination I could no longer hope, but had to accept the truth; I had seen and I suppose really had known the instant I had entered the church. Jack rushed past me as I fell to my knees, and the whole church resounded with my moan of anguish. Priest and farmer worked together in silence, gently lifting Thomas down and laying him on a pew. Father Umber came to m, but I was broken, shattered, numb and wanted to be left; to escape into another place. The priest persisted with his attention, and with his arm around me he lead me into the vestry. Father Umber began to tell me how everything had come about.

The captain of the soldiers had it in his head that there were rebels about, and his mission was to weed out such, and rid these parts of trouble. All father said just washed over me, I did not understand, or couldn't, we were just ordinary farming and shepherd folk; getting by as best we could. Nonetheless the outside world had invaded our peace, and murdered my husband. Why should he be killed in such a way; like a common felon? He had a good heart and a kind way. I could not fathom the terrible events.

I looked to Father Umber to try to understand why, but as I looked at him in the light of the vestry, my shock was worsened. My priest for as long as I could remember looked back, through blackened half closed eyes.

His nose was obviously broken, and blood had dried to a black crust on his swollen lips. He looked away as he told me how Dominic, though beaten, was safe and well enough. I sighed so deeply in relief, sobs stuttered on my mouth, in emotions so mixed in joy and despair.

Father Umber continued in the telling of events of that morn, in an atmosphere akin to confessional. He told me how he had been kept in the vestry under guard. After Bernadette had left earlier that morning, the Captain returned some hours later, followed by a platoon of redcoats dragging in Tom and Dominic. The Captain began to interrogate several men, but when he got no answers he ordered two of his men to beat Dominic. At first the lad had stood defiantly, but then, after further questions were met by silence, they weighed in again. At this Tom went berserk. He broke free from his guards, so enraged, killing one redcoat and gravely harming another. In moments he was overcome and laid out cold. Dispassionately, the captain had ordered the redcoats to lead the men out; and without even looking at Thomas, he ordered his men to hang him before leaving.

Father Umber had pleaded for mercy, but was just beaten unconscious, and when he came to he was greeted in his own parishby a vision so desperate his heart broke. The house of God, here on earth had been defiled by the cold-blooded killing of an innocent man. When my priest had finished telling me all; he sat back, closed his eyes and chanted prayers in Latin."

Barbara stopped talking and sighed heavily, she lifted her hands to her face and rubbed her eyes and forehead. No one in the room spoke, everyone just sat silently. We were all touched by everything we had heard, and the experience was so intense it affected each and every person who heard Barbara's heartfelt story.

The twilight magic of that moment was broken by a floor manager calling for the participants of the next show to go up to the filming area. The kitchen then sounded with chatter as everyone excitedly discussed what had passed.

"How are you?" I asked Barbara.

"Hhmm, tired!" she quietly answered.

"Do you remember what you were saying?" I asked with fascination.

"Yes I do, all of it," she smiled as she replied.

"There is a good chance over the next few days that more memories of that life will still come to you," I told her.

"Oh I hope so, I want to know what became of Mary," she sighed. Those were Barbara's final words before leaving that day.

Two weeks later I met Barbara again, it was at a workshop on past life recall. During the day she told me that no other memories had come to her. So after some discussion we decided to again try and access that same past life. I was aware that the difficulty at this stage was that, because some time had passed since the last session, reaching that particular incarnation may no longer be possible. In my many years of work with regression, I have come to understand that revealing past lives can be quite random; to arrive at a point of time in the past is not guaranteed.

What happened that day answered a lot of what Barbara wanted to know about Mary.

Once again, Barbara easily sank into a deep relaxation, the altered state of awareness. Straight away she began to mumble incoherently.

"Tell me your name," I prompted.

Again, she just mumbled.

"Speak to me clearly and loudly," I urged.

This was met by silence, but she was obviously seeing something as she was again showing signs of REM.

Again I tried,"Tell me your name."

"Mary," she eventually whispered her reply.

"Tell me what you see."

"Nothing," came the answer.

I was a little disappointed at this, even though the name was right, there was no coherence or clarity to the session.

"Mary, will you speak with me?" I tried.

"Yes," she answered, slowly moving her lips, giving the impression she was thirsty. "I am ready now, I have peace of mind and am confessed, absolved and cleansed."

"Tell me your name."

My command was to reaffirm her identity.

"Mary O' Caroll," she said again. I was glad to hear it.

"Tell me what you see, Mary."

"It's dark in here, except for a candle giving a little light over there," she sighed.

A smile came across her face, as she began to talk.

"Hello," she whispered.

Then as she spoke, Barbara began to sob softly; she lifted her hand as if to touch something. The 'hello' did not seem to be addressed to me.

"Is someone there?" I asked.

An expression crossed her face which seemed to suggest that she was a little annoyed by my interfering questions. She smiled again, becoming choked.

"It's my Thomas," she replied.

"Your husband?"

"Yes, he has come to take me with him, to be together…..together again."

It began to dawn on me, that we had arrived at a point in Mary's life close to her own death. Without any further prompting from me, Barbara commenced another speech:

"I can see a light in the corner of the room, I am lying in bed….I have been sick for some time with a coughing fever, and it is my time now. I am joyed by the sight of my family all with me, my lasses all grown to good women, and my son, a strapping lad, just like his dad. That was the only pain in my life, to lose my husband in such a cruel way. Many years have passed since that terrible time, when devils descended on our lives. We now live on the coast, looking out on the great ocean, with its waves either lapping at the shore, or storms crashing up the cliff face.

I love this place, so alive and so far away from that dreadful place where my heart had been scorched in hell's own furnace. My eyes are closing now, I can't see my family, but I can still hear them. It's dark now, but the light from the candle is growing brighter and my Thomas is here. I touch his face, it feels good. His eyes are bright and smiling at me, his lips so full, set in his handsome freckled face. I want to kiss him, to have him hold me again.

I can feel him lifting me in his strong arms, and carrying me from my sick bed. Before I know it I am walking with him, my arm linked into his. I feel well, young again, full of joy with a sense of love all around me.

We're strolling through an avenue of trees, so heavy with leaves they overlap above you, making an arched canopy. We have passed through the avenue and we are in a beautiful garden, ornamented with statues in white marble. There is every shade of green between the lawns and hedges sculpted in animal shapes, some of which I recognise but some are beyond me. He leads me through a maze until we come to a white-painted, wooden building, open on all sides. The building has five step-sized tiers leading onto a central platform, with a dozen or so men and women playing the most beautiful music.

All around me people are going about their business; talking, promenading and sitting at tables. Thomas leads me to a bench built into a lawn embankment, surrounded by beautiful flowers, the sound of the music harmonising with bird song on this marvelous sun-drenched day. Thomas pulls me close and kisses me gently on my lips. With my eyes closed we hold each other lightly, resting my head on his shoulder, I open my eyes to see lilac and white butterflies fluttering past. I can hear my son's voice somewhere in the distance saying ' goodbye ma', and now I know that I have not been dreaming some delirious fevered dream, but am safe in heaven and reunited with my love."

Barbara opened her eyes. She sat a little while without a word, as did everyone else. Eventually I took her hand, " Are you okay?" I asked. With a deep sigh of contentment she smiled and replied with genuine relief, "Fine".

Linda's Story

A Stormy Past

This particular story surprises many people, because Linda actually remembers a past life as a man.

The belief in reincarnation is as complex and varied as any belief system. The possibility of being reborn into every species here on earth is a view supported in several religions. Personally, I cannot find anything in my research to support this view. Perhaps the techniques of looking at past lives using only the human species limits the experiences we are to able to reach.

So I feel that as we are dealing with a subject that is hard enough to prove, it is best to concentrate on human possibilities only. I have come to learn that past lives are about experience, which is a learning for the soul. It follows that to live life fully, every possible lifestyle is necessary to understand every aspect of humanity.

I first met Linda at a demonstration of clairvoyance and past life recall at a hotel in Liverpool. Linda was among ten volunteers who wanted to take part in the demonstration of reincarnation.

During the evening several of the volunteers recalled a variety of previous lives, however, Linda claimed to see absolutely nothing. At the end of the evening Linda spoke to me as everyone was making their way out of the conference room. I realised she wanted privacy before she got to the crux of what was on her mind. The room seemed enormous once everyone left, with just the two of us still there.

" I'm sorry," she confessed.

"For what?" I asked, somewhat confused

"Well, when I said I'd seen nothing, that was not true, I just felt I could not talk."

"Why not?"

"I don't know, but I want to try again, if that's okay with you?"

"Of course, no problem, if that's what you want."

"When?" she asked.

I recommended that she should come to my next workshop, next month, letting her know that she just had to book her place. She seemed content with this.

"Bye, see you then," she smiled, turning to leave.

"Oh, by the way," I was still intrigued., "What did you see?"

"Fire and ice," was her enigmatic reply as she walked out.

The following month I was preparing for the workshop, laying out table and chairs in a circle. As always, I laid out name cards, one of which was Linda Trim, the young woman who had seen fire and ice. We ended a most interesting day in which several past life recalls had brought out remarkable events from the past. One in particular was very hard to believe, as it was set in the sea, and told of a great love between two souls who lived together as dolphins. I do not dismiss this recall completely, but I believe souls do not cross species. However, I can accept that sometimes, on a spiritual level, we can tune into thoughts from other intelligences besides humans.

Linda involved herself fully in the workshop that day, but nothing had surfaced. At the end of the session we all sat enjoying a cup of coffee and chatting about what had transpired that day.

"I know we're finished, and I'm sure you must to be keen to be going, but I'd really like to try once more," Linda suddenly ventured.

"No problem, I said, hoping I sounded enthusiastic, but really feeling tired and irritated.

Linda explained how when she had looked into the mirror during the session, all she had seen had been flames, although she felt icy cold.

I suggested that if we all put our thoughts into helping her 'see', the positive energy of a group of like-minded people would create an atmosphere of energy strong enough to possibly let Linda recall that past life, which was obviously present but still elusive.

We moved the tables away and arranged chairs in a circle around two in the middle, one for Linda and one for me. Linda sat in a dining chair, so her back was straight. Her eyes were closed and her feet bare so that she could earth herself to the ground through the plush hotel carpet. In her hands she clasped a piece of smoothly polished rose quartz tumble stone, about the size of a small egg. This particular piece of rose quartz was of two shades of pink; one half was quite a gentle milky rose that seemed to let no light through, the other half clearer, almost translucent, but full of flaws which created numerous rainbows as it split the light passing through it. She held crystal to her heart chakra (her sternum, at the centre of the chest) and I began to talk her through the process. Linda began to breathe deeply, inhaling through her nose and exhaling through her open mouth.

"Continue to breathe deeply and slowly," I said gently but firmly. "With each breath you will become more and more relaxed. Now imagine you see the light from the rose quartz beginning to infuse your aura with its beautiful pink light, but as you breathe out through your mouth, imagine you see your exhaled breath as a murky cloud, getting rid of all the negative energy. All the stress of the day, all of life's worries being breathed away. Continue to breathe deeply and slowly, in through nose and out through your mouth." I stopped talking for a short while to let her find her own rhythm, her own harmony. "Now take a big breath in through your nose and hold to the count of four, but when you breathe out, see your breath clear. You are now holding the rose quartz light at your heart chakra. Continue to breathe slowly and deeply."

I looked around the room and saw that everyone had closed their eyes and was breathing in rhythm, totally synchronised with Linda's breath, their chests rising and falling, creating a resonance of great harmony. I continued my instruction:

"Now let your consciousness drop from your head to your heart. See your chakra at your heart begin to spin and open. See the beautiful pink light swirl and draw energy up from the roots of your feet; at the same time, from the crown of your head, pulling in universal energy from the cosmos. Visualise all this energy being pulled into your heart chakra. As it spins, your consciousness becomes at one with your spiritual self."

I stopped for a short while and when I continued with this guided visualisation, I spoke a little more quietly:

"Now visualise a mirror in front of you, a full length dressing mirror. Look into the mirror and describe what you see. Begin at the bottom of the mirror and gradually lift your eyes until you have scanned the reflection in the mirror completely. Now tell me what you see."

I paused and waited for Linda to reply. She said nothing at first. She did, however, begin to hold herself more tightly as if she was feeling the cold.

Her teeth began to chatter and she sucked in her breath which whistled slightly between her dithering lips.

"I'm cold," she murmured.

"What do you see?" I urged.

"Fire," she moaned in reply.

I could see her obvious distress at what she was experiencing.

"At any time you can open your eyes and you will be back in this room. If you wish to continue, please do so, but speak to me clearly and loudly, you are quite safe, no matter what you see I am here with you all the time," I said, somewhat concerned.

As I spoke to her I put my hand on her shoulder to reinforce in her a sense of security.

"Fire, fire everywhere, I'm in the water, but the sea is on fire. I'm so tired, so cold. It doesn't hurt any more …my arm, I can't feel it."

"Where are you ?" I asked.

"Not sure, I know we were on our way to Singapore, until we were hit and now the old girl is sunk," she tried to explain.

This was incredible. If what I was perceiving was right, Linda was remembering a past life which was quite recent, possibly the Second World War. It also occurred to me that she could be remembering a past life as a man, most likely a sailor. My concern was that she seemed to be seeing the end of that life, so eliciting more information seemed difficult.

"Tell me your name," I insisted.

"David," she stated.

"Is anyone with you David?" I asked.

"Yes, Jed, but he's dead now," came the abrupt reply.

"What did you say?" I persisted.

"Jed is dead, I think everyone is, I don't know why I'm not," she uttered.

"How long have you been in the water?"

"Don't know, I don't feel well."

" That's okay, relax, you're safe," I said, trying to be reassuring.

"No I'm not …I can't get away."

Linda seemed to weaken, falling silent after her outburst. I had decided that it would be wise to end the session, and was about to bring Linda out of her Heart, light, Harmony State, when she started to talk again.

"I must get away, I need to swim under the flames, but I can't go under, this bloody lifesaver. I can't get the sodding thing off!"

Again she abruptly stopped talking.

"David, can you hear me?" I asked, not wanting to lose 'him'.

"Yes," came the distracted voice.

"David, can you tell me what is happening?" I spoke with some urgency, watching for any signs on Linda's face. At that moment I became aware of the rest of the group, watching just as intently, all of them sitting on the edge of their chairs.

After a pause, with an enormous gap, Linda spat the words out:

"I'm free, clear of the flames, I managed to get the jacket off, and I swam under the flaming water," she panted.

"David, are you okay?"

"Yes," she gasped.

"David, tell me what you can see," I demanded.

"Smoke and fire on the water, filling the sky, but there are no boats, no ships, they are all gone or sunk."

"Can you see anyone else around you?" I tried to open out the entire scene.

"No, no one, I'm all alone, I must swim but it's hard, I'm tired, I feel weak," she again gasped for air. She sighed and blew her cheeks out, before falling silent once more.

"David, speak to me, David," I said encouragingly.

"I can't," Linda whispered weakly. "I ...I can't, I'm going under."

I could just about hear her faint words. Then suddenly she shouted out.

"Mam!" she yelled.

"David, can you hear me?" I tried again.

"Yes."

The answer was clear but the voice was somehow different, something intangible, but definitely different.

Linda opened her eyes. She was breathless, like someone after tremendous exertion, gasping for oxygen to go back into the body.

"Gosh!" she exclaimed, before going on to tell of how she had felt and experienced everything. Now she remembered what David was thinking even after his death. She explained:

"David had become overcome by fatigue and his weary body could no longer fight the sea. It was pulling him down into a watery grave. His lungs were burning in pain as he tried to hold his breath, but it was to no avail, his lips parted under the pressure, and a rush of carbon dioxide bubbled out of his mouth and nose. He closed his mouth again, but in seconds he reopened it involuntarily and the salt water rushed in, flooding his lungs. He thrashed his legs and right arm, his left arm having been blasted away when an explosion had thrown him from the ship.

The sea was dragging his body deeper and deeper into the abyss. Bereft of light, with eyes bulging, giving an impression of horror, but in fact life had already gone, and all sensation in his body had ended. David plummeted to the sea bed at such speed that it seemed as if some invisible plug had been pulled, creating massive suction on his cadaver. The downward velocity seemed impossible."

Her description was so vivid and intense that I was able to visualise the whole horrific scene. She continued to describe the events. "At the same time as this dreadful scene, a magnificent light burst out of David's chest and formed itself into a beautiful sub-aqua angel, that soared through the waves and transformed into a shooting star crossing the sky westward."

Linda paused before carrying on, "David,s mind and mine had melded so that I was experiencing his life and thoughts completely. However, he was unaware of me. His name was David Ho, born in Liverpool in a small terraced house just off Scotland Road to an English mother and a Chinese merchant seaman, who still had family in Shanghai. The young master Ho had enjoyed his childhood playing in the street between Great Homer Street and the dock road.

By the time that David was nine he earned pennies working in a Chinese cook house in Cleveland Square. It was there that he became enticed by stories of China and seafarers. Throughout his formative years he absorbed not just an understanding of oriental food but also of the philosophy of Eastern life. During those years he developed a quick mind, despite his frequent truancies from school!

After drowning, David's body was lying at the bottom of the sea and was surely nourishment for the aquatic creatures, scavenging on the prolific human windfall."

Linda again paused. She complained of a dry throat and asked for a glass of orange juice with Vodka. Once fortified with the fruit drink laced with alcohol, she continued with her recollection of this fascinating previous life.

"I have already told you how our minds had joined together in a way that gave me complete understanding of his thoughts. With what happened next it was hard to decipher whether it was memory or real experience. I was walking along a dark street as though I was David and yet I did not exist."

Linda again paused and sipped her drink, before continuing.

"The street I was in was familiar, but very dark and the rain, now stopped, must have been heavy as the flags and cobbles shone in their wetness. The next instant I was stooped at the quayside, looking across the Mersey which was full of ships and tugs. There were no electric lights, just stars and a crescent moon illuminated the river and Wirral bank. As clouds broke up to clear the night sky, I sat on a capstan and just watched the world go by in silent darkness.

As dawn came I found myself strolling along Wapping, but as I reached Chinatown the smell of cooking was so enticing that it drew me in it's direction and there, among the towering mills and warehouses, was a hut. The hut was a cobbled- together shanty, crowded with a group of oriental men enjoying breakfast as they stood around. They all held bowls in their left hands close to their mouths as they shovelled in rice and fried salt fish with chop sticks in their right hands.

There was something wrong with what I was seeing, as everything was just memories, but I did not remember this particular cookshop. The cooked food was not as interesting as I remembered, no fish dumpling, no pork, no chow mien or my favourite, duck. So even though it smelt wonderful, I was not tempted. The next moment I was in Scotland Road and people were now filling the road, going about their business. I decided to go home, but somehow I ended up in Rose Hill and walked past the police station, which gave me a shiver as I recalled the scrapes I'd gotten into as a child. 'A little rapscallion' one bobby had called me as his large hand had swiped me across the side of my head, nearly taking it off. I could still feel that clout as I walked on.

I turned away as I saw constable McGrath coming my way with his ruddy face and lean figure in his uniform, he made a formidable sight. He was probably a very nice man; but looked constantly angry and constipated. I tried not to run past him, watching the pavement, not daring to look up. In my need to move on quickly, I nearly ran into a fruit and vegetable barrow being pushed by a woman who was perhaps not so old, but looked hard done by. She was Dolly Hickey, who had a kind way, but also a bark and equally sharp bite. She seemed to look straight through me as I skipped around her, and when I stopped and looked back she had parked her barrow. She talked with the policeman as he polished an apple against his sleeve. I feared they were talking about me, so I turned on my heels and headed home.

I reached the top of my street and began to make my way to my house. Once outside my front door I hesitated and as I searched my pockets I found I had no key. In fact my pockets were empty, no money or anything.

I was about to knock on the door when it opened. A man I did not know appeared and stepped past me, and without a word he was gone. He had left the door open, so even though I was a little puzzled I walked in, calling out. I moved down the dark hall; the gas mantles were set low and the parlour door was closed, but the back room door was open. As I entered, there was a glow from the range where the kettle was just boiling, the sound of a holly leaf rattling inside. The mantles were also set low in this room, letting the firelight dominate and create exaggerated shadows around the walls. My mam was sitting in an upholstered rocking chair, positioned between the range and back window, which had heavy, drawn curtains, hiding a bleak back yard.

My eldest sister lifted the kettle and began to fill a teapot, set on a square table with an embroidered cloth, upon which four places were set. Mam seemed to be sleeping, whilst May was busy preparing tea. All looked normal, just how I remembered the home of my childhood, but they were taking no notice of me, just back from the high seas. At that thought, my head began to spin, it seemed they could not see me, but what I saw was not memories, it was real. I shouted at the top of my voice 'It's me David, I'm home, mam'.

They still took no notice, I was obviously invisible to them, either that or dreaming the whole episode. I tried to steady myself and sat in the only armchair, taking in everything in the compact room. Above the black grate and cooking range was a mantelpiece adorned with several ornaments and a clock. Above this the King and Queen watched over my family from their picture, which was surrounded by the union flag. The walls hosted many plaques depicting, in relief, Chinese images, including a brightly coloured rooster for the present year. There was, however, one plaque out of place; a deep relief depicting a landscape, showing a flowing river with a watermill on its bank. The flickering of the fire and the moving shadows caused the water wheels to move as I watched the plaque, which bore the legend 'Shannon'. I was becoming hypnotised by the unusual picture in plaster, when the man who had gone out leaving the door open earlier, returned carrying a steaming, newspaper-wrapped parcel, and the wonderful smell of fish and chips filled the room.

I jumped to my feet and at that moment he put the paper-wrapped supper down on the table and walked around the table on his way to the scullery. As he came towards me, I was moving out of his way, but he turned in my direction. Instantly we collided, but instead of being knocked to the ground, I shivered from my head to my toes. He passed straight through me and shuddered, pronouncing that he felt as though someone had walked over his grave.

From that moment on I knew what had been happening. These were not memories or dreams of my life, but I was a lost soul, a spectator, roaming through the places I held precious. I was still in the room, or at least in my mind, my consciousness was. I was just floating in mid air, my body seemed to be no more. As we colided the shudder I felt was followed by a vibration, a resonance that caused my whole being to fracture and splinter. The event disorientated me, causing a sensation of nausea and then I was non-corporeal, just thought, but I could see what had happened to my ghost of a body. It had become thousands upon thousands of minute droplets, like an infinitesimally fine rain spreading out, then popping into brilliant colours, creating a rainbow within the room.

Without physically possessing eyes, I could still see everything in the room, but I could feel a pull as though I was being drawn away. The last thing I was aware of was my mam being nudged out of her nap to have her fish supper. As she took her place at the table, Mam told how she had just had a lovely dream that David had come home and was sitting in father's chair. They were all silent, and I could just make out May standing up with tears filling her eyes. She turned up the gas mantle, wiped her face and bluntly changed the subject, declaring 'we can see what we are eating now!'

Then I was surrounded by a light so brilliant that it should have been unbearable, but it wasn't. In fact I felt wonderful, happy, even elated. Just wonderful, yes, wonderful. Once my emotion had calmed a little, I realised that I had a body once more, or perhaps it just felt like I had.

I was sitting on a wooden floor, not any ordinary floor, it was gleaming and the boards were laid so neatly that the grain continued through the joints unbroken, creating a floor that looked like it was made from one piece of sublimely ground wood. Getting to my feet and looking around, what surrounded me was breathtaking. I was standing in an enormous ballroom without walls. Colonnades of marble supported a ceiling draped with silver and gold-coloured silk and satin, pleated and interwoven and glistening from the light of the crystal chandeliers that hung majestically from the ceiling. The central chandelier, the king of crystal light, dominated the ballroom. This beautiful centre of light was accompanied by smaller, but equally spectacular chandeliers spread out in a spiral to the edge of this circular ballroom. Its classical pillars opened out to a view of stunning blue sky.

I walked to the edge of the shining room and touched the marble pillar, which felt surprisingly warm. It dawned on me as I touched the marbel, that I now had both my hands, my body was entirely whole and well again. Questions of how? what? and why? Ran through my head. I assumed that I must be dead and that this must be heaven.

I looked up. It was neither day or night, the sky was a rich blue with a bright sun; but there was also a full moon and stars, myriads of stars, bright and sparkling. Looking down there was no earth, just beautiful sky all around. The pillared ballroom was floating in the air, although it was quite still, with no wind or movement.

Quite literally out of nowhere, a star began to vibrate, blink and swirl, before bursting open to form a brilliant golden cloud. The cloud moved towards me, I stepped back and as I did so the cloud entered the ballroom. In front of me, as I stood there with wide open eyes and dropped jaw, this magical mist slowly began to contract and form into a beautiful young woman. The vision in front of me was exceptionally moving, she was radiant and had an aura of peace about her. I felt that I knew her. She took my hand and it felt so good, familiar even. I was about to ask her who she was, but she stopped me by putting her hand to my mouth.

I felt dizzy, unsteady on my feet, then suddenly I was back in that terraced street of my childhood, outside my family home. 'What ...?' I whispered in confusion but before I could force the rest of the question, my companion at my side hushed me. Still holding hands she led me to the other side of the street and we just stood there looking at my house. I remember thinking to myself, 'Why are we just standing here?' Then a new thought entered my head, but it felt like nothing I had ever thought before. It was new, unfamiliar, different and almost voice-like. This thought was telling me that we had come to visit my mother.

I looked to my beautiful companion holding my hand to help me to understand and she was looking intently back at me. Her eyes were so bright and it seemed impossible that such dark brown, almost black, eyes could radiate such startling light. Her gaze moved from me to the other side of the street. I followed the direction of her gaze, to see the door of my house open and watch my sister May step out. That loud thought was there again in my head. After a moment of confusion my mind found an incredible clarity; May was not my sister, she was my mam."

At that Linda blinked her eyes open. We all just sat in absolute silence for a few moments, without making a single motion. Then the intensity of the emotional experience overwhelmed Linda and she began to weep. Instantly everyone moved to embrace her. Everyone present had been touched by this special and significant experience and I will never forget the depth of emotion we felt that night.

Alan's Story

What Goes Around Comes Around

I had been invited to take part in an evening of clairvoyance and my contribution was to be a demonstration of past life regression. That particular evening was one of those hot, humid August nights, with the air so still that even open windows and doors in the packed hall could not ease the audience's discomfort.

The atmosphere of that evening was not conductive to regression, as my volunteers were being lulled to sleep by the oppressive atmosphere, rather than entering into a deep relaxing state of altered awareness.

The nocturnal heat had sapped everyone's energy, so I brought my quest for past lives to a premature conclusion. The volunteers were stirred from their public sleep and returned to the audience in anticipation of the next demonstration of mediumship. All but one had left the platform. I placed my hand on his right shoulder and repeated the words that would remove his altered state.

As I concluded with "Now open your eyes", he turned his head towards me, screwed up his face and with his eyes closed he spat at me, thankfully missing. Once he had expelled his venom in my direction his face turned to a mischievous smile, lighting up his classical, handsome face. This disarming grin was accompanied by a blast of what seemed to be obscenities, alas my understanding of them was only guessed at.

Then, the man opened his eyes. Gasping, he clasped his hand over his mouth and at the same time his cheeks flushed with embarrassment. He released the grip on his mouth while staring at me in sheer disbelief.

"I'm so sorry. I didn't mean to, I couldn't help myself," he stammered.

His eyes gave away the fact that he recognised that I was watching him as much as listening to what he said. Something in my expression alerted him to think me doubtful of what had happened. He need not have worried, his countenance and expression had been real not feigned, and his obvious embarrassment was a genuine reaction to his public mortification. The hall was silent, only a chair creaked. An almost tangible stillness invaded the hall, everyone had become transfixed. The temperature seemed to lower as a communal shiver instantly touched each one of us, cascading through the atmosphere to bring a refreshing coolness.

"How do you feel?" I asked the troubled man.

"Not sure ...I mean, I'm okay, it's just when you started talking us through, all I could see was a wall," he offered, in an attempt to explain his obviously out-of-character behaviour.

"A wall?" I echoed.

"Yes, a great stone wall, but I was up so close to it that it filled my view, then I suddenly felt very angry, enraged. I was seething with hatred and when you were speaking to me I thought you were a sheriff's man," he explained, puzzled.

"I suggest we leave it now, but later we can continue, if that's what you want," I suggested in a whisper. Then I turned to address the audience, "Thank you for your attention, as you can see we have had little success this evening. So I let the medium for the evening begin her demonstration, once again I thank you."

Once back in the committee room, away from the audience, which I felt sure was disappointed, I sighed with relief. Alan was already sitting there.

"Tea, or something stronger?" enquired Jean, a developing medium and general girl Friday, who always seemed so enthusiastic about everything.

"Tea would be fine," Alan meekly replied.

I took my tea and went into the garden, Alan followed.

"Could murder a pint," he declared, smacking his lips. After a moment he said, "There was something else as well, I didn't realise at first, but now I understand. As well as the wall, I was manacled in chains and afraid, scared, really scared for my life …" he paused.

The summer evening was changing from a twilight hue, to an orange, purple with scarlet streaks, crowned with a starry, moonless navy.

"Why do we think ourselves so important, when we are so small, so insignificant against that?" Alan asked, to no one in particular.

He seemed to be making a statement, rather than asking a question, as he looked towards the northern night sky.

"Yes, it does seem so, nonetheless even though we are a very small planet, we are many millions of souls, and in the scheme of things we are important. Despite our enormous numbers, each and everyone is uniquely special," I offered.

"I'm a sceptic, of course, not really into all this. I just came along with my girlfriend," he shrugged.

"That's okay, we shouldn't blindly just accept everything that's presented to us. What I do is to show a possibility of past lives, not to prove anything one way or the other," I explained to him.

"I know I didn't see much, but I felt a lot and it was real, not imagined." He chewed his lip in concentration, then continued. "I want you to put me under again."

"There's no need," I responded.

"Pardon?" Alan asked in confusion.

I explained further: "It's all there already, you just have to relax and let it all bubble up to the surface. What you have said about how you felt suggest that the memories of the past life are there, ready for the telling."

By this time the final demonstration had finished and people were emerging from the hall. Some of them came into the garden and congregated around the koi carp pond in silent contemplation, a cascade of coins had been thrust into the fountain rim of the centre of the pond as hopeful wishes were made. Then, many of them left to make their way home. Several matches were struck into flames and cigarettes glowed red, lighting up satisfied faces as they walked away from the fountain bearing the legend ` Cancer Appeal Fund`.

"Now that's what I call faith!" he grinned at his observation.

"Come," I invited him to take a seat at a plastic patio set. We were joined by Alan's girlfriend and a few others who had tuned into what was about to happen.

I asked Alan to make himself comfortable and close his eyes. He relaxed quickly and was breathing deeply, his closed eyes showed REM. Only a few moments had passed when a distinct change came across his face. His gentle, easy way seemed to now be hard, even angry and his smile was still there, but was now somehow menacing. I could swear his hair had a slight curl and greasiness that I had not noticed before.

"Can you hear me?" I asked, but Alan just tossed about in his chair and grimaced.

"Will you speak to me?" I tried again.

"Let me out!" Alan suddenly shouted. "Oh God, let me free."

"Speak to me," I urged.

"Nah!" he dismissively spat out the word.

"Why not?"

"I don'na know thee," was the reply.

"Do not worry, you can trust me," I firmly reassured him.

He shrugged his shoulders and chuckled sarcastically."I thus they think me a fool, be pissed on spy."

This intelligible rebuff was followed by peels of sneering laughter that made my spine tingle.

Then Alan opened his eyes and gasped, "Wow!" he marvelled.

"Are you okay?" I asked

"Yes,brilliant, gosh. I tell you, if I could have got at you I'm sure I would have choked you!"

"What do you mean?" I checked uncomfortably.

"It was so real, incredible. I was there, completely. Listen I'm an accountant, logical and scientifically minded. I know what I experienced was genuine, not a dream or a trick of the imagination."

"So why did you want to choke me?" I had to ask.

"I thought you were an inquisitor, or some kind of agent provocateur trying to trick me."

"So what else do you remember?" I encouraged him.

"I think I know him, I'm not ready to believe that was me in a previous life, even though it seemed very real. Nonetheless I shall keep an open mind."

"That's all I ask, now can you tell me more?" I carried on.

"Yes, though I'm not quite sure where to start. I suppose at the point I came in."

Alan lifted his cup and looked down at the dregs.

"Would like a glass of water?" Jean asked.

"I suppose so, though I'd rather have a pint!" he again joked.

"No problem," Jean reached under her chair and produced, as if performing a conjuring trick, a four pack of chilled beer. The click and hiss of ring pulls was followed by appreciative ` aahhs`!

From a copse at the bottom of the garden an owl could be heard hooting, adding to the eeriness of this nocturnal moot concerned with Alan's past life recall.

"It seems the wise one from the wood is ready to listen as well, so when you're ready, let's hear all," I began.

Alan sat back, closed his eyes and began to take deep, slow breaths, like a practised shaman. He had become comfortable with his paradox.

Without any questions being asked, Alan began to transform again, his face started its exercise of expressions as his previous incarnation unfolded in his mind. He began to mumble under his breath, then slowly the odd word became clear. It was Latin, parts of prayers or a mass. Tears were in his eyes as they opened, although he was still in a trance-like state.

"Mea Culpa, Mea culpa," he repeated several times, with other words I could not attune to.

Then he sighed and slumped forward. In the next moment he sat up straight again, completely awake and alert.

"I've seen the other side," he smiled the words out, laughing freely,intoxicated by the experience.

His laughter became infectious. So before I got caught up in inexplicable merriment, I broke the inappropriate party mood.

"Well?" I enquired loudly.

The silence was instant, but fragile. Like disobedient children, those present held their breath, biting on their lips to suppress the giggles that were waiting to burst out.

"Well, what happened?" I demanded.

With sudden sobriety Alan looked me in the eye and began his reply.

"They hung, hee, hee, ho hung me." Was all he managed, before he became helplessly, hopelessly stricken by more laughter, along with everyone else, including myself. What is more, he continued through the laughter to repeat what had happened.

"The bastards hung me, the bastards!" he yelped almost hysterically.

Then the laughter abruptly ceased. His expression altered and his smiles turned to tears.

"Are you okay?" I asked with concern.

"Yes, fine. Sorry, it's just that so much emotion ran through me," he explained.

"What do you remember?" I asked, trying to concentrate his mind.

"Everything, even being in heaven. That was amazing. I also remember all the pain, a life that was hell on earth, but I knew no better."

He continued as if in a confessional, pouring it all out.

"Jack was my, er, his name, well you know what I mean. Just Jack, I'm not aware of any family name, or any family or blood relative, but I was getting baptised I know that. I remember getting away as a small boy from an abbey. I don't know when or what age I was, or where it was.

After some days away, hunger and fear nearly drove me back. Then I came across people living in the woods. They were hardy, rough folk, unkind and unwelcoming. I sat behind tall grass watching them. They had seen me, but for the most part ignored me, after literally throwing stones or sticks at me.

Several days had passed, and I had survived on scraps of food that I would steal as they slept. Thankfully that summer was warm, so looking after myself was none too difficult. Each day I would move a little closer, until shouts and stares came my way and I would retreat quickly. One night their fires were burning less brightly than usual and no men could be seen, only the women and their children, some smaller and just two taller than me. As I watched, the smell of food caused my eyes to cry as hunger made me sick with pain. I wanted to go to them and ask for some food. Suddenly a woman came out of nowhere. I jumped back, with my heart pounding and beating like it was near its end. I wanted to run but panic pinned me where I was.

She held out her hand and upon it was some burnt earth with something else, I know not what, but it smelled wonderful. I looked from her hand to her face, it was old and dirty with a toothless mouth and rancid breath. Fear still gripped me. I only stared at her, although I wanted to grab what she offered me from her hand. She mumbled words which meant nothing to me, then placed the rustic makeshift earth dish down. As she moved away, I scooped it up and quickly consumed all, without understanding what I tasted, but when I finished I could see pieces of pine needles, embedded into the earth dish.

I later discovered that I had actually eaten the meat of a hedgehog and from then onwards it seemed that I was part of the group. I was the lowest of the low in the pack for the first few years, but I learned quickly and made myself useful and became big enough to lay out anyone who tried to beat me. So there I was living amongst the Wolf Heads and the Footpads, with many scars and deformities of mind and body caused by the brutality of life, a life I now embraced."

Alan paused and stretched with a long yawn of fatigue.

"Are you tired?" I checked.

"Yes - but I want to get it all out, all that I remember. I don't want to stop."

It was now past midnight, so Jean made coffee and settled once again, Alan continued.

"Though we were like family, no one really cared or felt for anyone else. We stayed together out of self preservation, not respect, well, except for Don. Don was very much the leader, physically strong and without regard for anyone. If he wanted anything, he took it, be it large or small. So through fear he was respected as the leader, what he said was never challenged. Over the years I learned to be unnoticed, unimportant; it seemed those closest to him suffered all the more.

One day, despite my efforts to remain inconspicuous, I was called on by Don. He wanted me to lead a raid over on the other side of the moors. I think I was given this job just because of that reason, it was another county, in the area of another Wolf Head chief. So the danger was not just from the militia but also rivals.

It took three days to journey into the county of York, but we knew it would be worth it. Our prey was a manor house, lightly guarded as the master and his men were in service to their lord, leaving only women and old folk to put aside before taking a goodly profit in riches. Don had learned this from one he called ` a trusty fellow`. The return journey would be easy, as we would find good horse stock.

The arrival at the manor was not well met, we had for some miles carefully trudged through wood and thicket in which there was a faint smell of smoke. Once we broke cover, the reason for the fumes was apparent; the manor, surrounding buildings and homes had been laid waste. As the realisation of what was before us dawned on me, the still quiet of disappointment was broken by the racket of men bearing down on us. Despite our usual stealth we were being ambushed, beaten and left for dead.

After some time I was once again in my senses. Oddly, my strong fellows in mischief were also battered and bruised, but alive, if not well. It seemed our assailants were perhaps other Wolf Heads, intent on giving a lesson in boundaries rather than the kill. We mustered to apprise the situation and found three of the seven of us were able to stand and continue, if somewhat gingerly. The remaining four retreated, taking cover to lick their wounds. Leaving our battered and bloody comrades, we hobbled towards what remained of the smouldering manor house. Most ordinary good and God-fearing folk would feel horrified and sickened by what we found; no one was left alive or unspoiled. The killing was not enough for these Wolf Heads; the evidence of rape and sodomy was evident on the battered remains of the brutalised dead. What made this all the worse was the knowledge that my fellow robbers and I would and did act no better.

I suppose it was then that I realised what I had become, a selfish beast only concerned with myself. The memories buried so deeply in me suddenly rose to the surface, I slumped at the reality of what I was part of. My fellow Footpads only cursed their misfortune at losing such a prize to another bunch of parasites. Within moments it dawned on us that we dare not return empty- handed to Don. We had spent some time talking through our grim options as we returned to our comrades.

Before we reached cover and our comrades, the hue and cry of horsemen, some dozen or so,emerged from the woodlands. This time we were surely done for. These were no rabble, but sheriff's militia; hard, professional warriors, who had seen service in battle. I expected no mercy and was ready to walk with the reaper. To my astonishment they held their ground awhile, and keeping us under shrewd eyes, they gradually surrounded us. Within so short a time it seemed impossible, we were manhandled and manacled. A sergeant began to interrogate my fellows and I, and it became obvious they saw us as part of the despicable pack who had so disgracefully attacked this household. No protest from us would persuade them otherwise, so I kept myself silent, despite the beatings.

As the day turned towards night it became apparent that we were for the noose at York. Sleep may well have been impossible that night, were it not for the ash staff I saw swung in my direction, before startling lights of pain were followed by a blackness that took away my senses.

The following morning I was roused without a pause to attend to my personal needs. I and my two companions, shackled together, were marched onward. On the march we were closed in north, south, east and west by sturdy, attentive horsemen, escape was not an option.

On that long march I had time to think and think I did. What had happened to our four battered comrades hiding in the wood? Had they been slain, did they escape? To ask would be pointless, as they were obviously not here and enquiry could add to their danger, if free they be. Thinking every part of my life over,and over again, I had begun to severely curse my past bad judgement and misfortune. Suddenly I was inside the city walls, so lost in my self pitying reverie that the reality of where I was shocked my body and mind cold. Terror immobolised me and I actually soiled myself, but it mattered not, my revolting stench was no worse than that of my low company. After all, we had been proud to be seen as wolves in combat, and so to be treated as animals now was no great hardship. To be hanged for someone else's deed did not seem unfair or unjust, as the crime they had done was only what we intended, so perhaps that was just. Anyway, I was far from innocent, I had robbed, battered and killed enough to warrant a hanging. I had chosen this life; I had abandoned the cloister to be free.

My mind was split. If this was how I felt, then why did I feel so bad? Why did I want with all my fiber to protest? I had actually had no part in what happened at that manor. Yet I was still a murderer, a looter. I cared not a jot for any others and it was my own actions that had brought me to this place. Caught red-handed - or so they believed - but the red blood on my hand was not for that crime. They saw us as evil villains who rob, kill and spoil. That was what I could not be held responsible for. Many things I was, but a spoiler of women and children I was not. Yet along with my other crimes, I would be damned, damned to Hell. So I began to wish to be at the gallows pole quickly, in the hope that maybe death would be an end, a descent into a bleak abyss where my mind and thoughts would be dead forever, never to be resurrected.

The gallows did not come quickly, even though I languished in a fetid dungeon cell. I knew that more than one full day had passed. The coming and goings of other persons marked out some of the time. I spent the time with my face to a cold, damp wall with its own world of tiny flora and fauna. I became intoxicated by fear and a stench so pervasive, it made my empty stomach retch. Though than two days had passed without food, I felt no hunger and the water we shared was brackish, so thirst was also ignored.

I began to escape into my past, my childhood among the brothers and friends at the abbey. I was dazed and confused. My present state, my life of late and the abbey life of a child were all merging into a thick haze. The pain of hunger was not enough to sober me. Without any thoughts of my actions, I began to beat my chest as hard as I could, whilst mumbling my confession and the mantra Mea Culpa. As I gazed blankly at the wall, it seemed to lose its solidity and began to shimmer, and dance crazily backwards and forwards. No matter how hard I tried to focus on one point, the stone would not rest in one place. The sound of angelic voices chanting canticles, remembered from my vespers at the abbey, resounded in my head as my legs gave way and I swooned out of consciousness.

My recovery back to reality was no blessing; as my senses came under control once more, I realised that I had been stripped. Several gaolers were roughly washing me under the supervision of a priest. My instinct was to fight this unexpected cleansing, but as I weakly tried to twist myself free, I was rewarded with a hard blow to my mouth. I was then marched, totally naked, to another cell which, although bare and austere, was at least clean, having lime-washed walls and floor.

The priest followed and in his arms he carried a bundle of clothes. He told me to dress. What I put on were no more than rags, but at least they were clean. He told me quite coldly: ` You came into this world innocent and clean, so it is my duty to ensure that, though not innocent, you will be shriven and clean when you meet your maker'. He then knelt down as he clasped his hands in prayer and invited me to do likewise and confess and repent.

I was incensed that this so-called man of God assumed my guilt without question. He was like brethren with whom I had spent years as a child, demanding confessions followed by penance. My confessions then were my own imaginings. Today they were in part his imagining. Nonetheless, I would confess because I felt guilty of so many other crimes, what did it matter that I was not guilty of the deed which I would swing for? The priest gave absolution, then left, muttering something to a gaoler as he passed him.

The gaoler then beckoned me to follow him. I did so, in an almost dream-like state as we climbed tower steps until we reached an open door which led to a chamber which was totally dark. I entered without being told. It was cold and dark, the only light coming from a sconce torch outside the door. The gaoler left, leaving the door open. I just stood there in the darkness, cold, afraid and feeling utterly alone. I sensed something - the smell of horses, of sweat, of the stable. I thought I could hear breathing.

I wanted to call out 'Who's there?', but fear froze my throat. I could neither talk nor move. I eventually took hold of my senses again, and moved to the door. Suddenly, my nerve was shattered. I let out a scream as the doorway was filled by the figure of an enormous man silhouetted in front of me. The strong smell of horses and the sweat of a hard ride was on him. 'The Lord may be satisfied with your bastard corpse, but only after I have done with thee,' he spat loudly. I felt no fear, but I knew what was about to happen. I had little time to dwell as pain invaded my eye, then exploded into intolerable agony, and my whole body shook with the simultaneous bite of fire and ice. Time lost its meaning as all that was done to me happened at an unbearably slow pace. My instinct was to fight back, but this became impossible as my limbs were twisted and pulled until sinew and bone stretched and broke. My chest and back were beaten until the ribs audibly cracked. My body lay on the floor, misshapen but unbloodied, apart from my face which no longer held my eyes. The blindness did not matter, nor did my broken body. Oddly, the coolness of the fetid chamber floor suited me as my right cheek pressed into it, supporting my newly deformed self. I began to lose consciousness, but before I slid away from the situation, I felt and smelt hot water spatter my face, as my assailant and his henchmen emptied their bladders over me.

The unconsciousness that began to envelop me suddenly evaporated and I was immediately and completely alert, not in my own body, but actually standing beside and outside myself. I could actually see my own broken and crumpled body lying in a heap on the floor, with lungs fighting for breath. I was therefore watching this scene, not dreaming, not dreaming at all; there but not there.

The avengers left without a word or expression exchanged, silently, stealthily, they disappeared into the depths of the gaol. The gaolers dragged my broken body out and as they did so, were discussing whether or not I would be fit for hanging that morning, or just cast into the lime pit.

I was free of my body. I could see all that was happening, yet I stayed close by. I felt I could just float away - a spirit free to meet my Maker. However, I chose not to, but felt compelled to remain with my poor, pathetic, battered body.

Then a thick, overpowering tiredness overcame me. I tried to stay alert, to keep vigil on myself, but it was impossible. I was sucked into blackness and all thought was gone.

I returned to consciousness to hear the sound of voices, many voices, though the words indistinct, chattering in the distance. I was still in blackness punctuated by splashes of colour - red, blue, purple, green appearing for no reason. Then the pain hit me. My whole body was a pulse of never - ending pain. Despite not having any vision, I knew exactly what was happening. I was being lashed to a board and a hood was being placed over my head. The nightmare I was remembering was no dream of evil, but was true. I was for the gallows. I had been beaten senseless, broken in my limbs, and my eyes gouged out. The events had caused my spirit to flee my body, but now, though broken and blinded, I was in my wits once more, as I was forced to the gallows.

I felt myself being shuffled into position. This act alone was enough to kill me. The agony of the movement caused me to cry, cry like I was a child again. My crying somehow had an effect on the watching crowd. Though I could not see, I felt, as well as heard, the anger and bitterness in them, they jeered, shouted and even laughed as the noose was positioned around my neck. Death could not come quickly enough. I felt the rope tighten against my left ear, forcing my head to tilt to the right. I wanted it to end. I seemed to be waiting an eternity. Suddenly, I swung out to the sound of my neck cracking - then the pain was over.

I was out of myself again, but this time I just floated free, and did not look back, just ascended into the sky."

Seemingly drained, Alan then fell silent for some time all that could be heard was his deep, rhythmic breathing. Then his face seemed to glow as a wonderful smile lit it up.

"This is wonderful - just wonderful!"

He said the words through a happy smile.

"What is wonderful?" I asked, captivated

"I just feel so good, happy, very pleased," he beamed.

"Where are you?" I probed.

"I am standing on a riverbank, looking across the river to the other side. It's a wide river. I can see a wooden jetty just below me, and there's a small rowing boat tied up. There's a man in the boat, but his back is towards me so I can't see his face. He's dressed in a shabby habit. As I watched him on a beautiful fine day with no breeze, so the rich white clouds hang motionless like whipped meringue fixed in a summer blue sky, he turns towards me and beckons me to come over.

I make my way to the jetty, and by the time I step onto the boards, he is already in the boat with boards resting across his lap. With his hands he invites me onto the boat. As I step on, he points to the rope which ties the boat to the jetty. Instinctively, I untie the rope and take my seat on a board that creaks as I sit facing him. The hood of his habit is now up. I realise that I had taken no notice of his face, and all I can see now under his habit are his even, white teeth as he grins with strain, pulling on the oars, so that the boat moves out into the river."

Alan's face showed obvious relief as he carried on. "I sat still and watched his mouth and double chin move back and forth under the shadow cast by his heavy hood. I didn't ask where we were going - I just felt contented and peaceful.

The river was still and passive, even the stroke of the oars hardly disturbed the water as we glided smoothly along. Trees became more plentiful on both banks as we sailed up the river. Bulrushes stood to attention, protecting the wildlife of the river bank. As we navigated a bend, my by now sweaty, rotund oarsman pulled our little vessel towards a grotto, erected by heavily leaning willows stretching their trailing branches into the water. As we entered the natural cave, birds, butterflies and two swans lazily moved out. Despite their exit, a symphony of the riverside fauna filled the air with a comforting ambient harmony.

My boatman, now breathless, pulled back his hood to reveal a red, hot face, which broke into a generous smile with laughing eyes of the lightest green. I was surprised at how young he was. I had expected an old man, I suppose. I was even more surprised to feel that something about him seemed familiar. I felt I knew him and he also seemed to know me.

In one smooth movement, he leapt from the boat onto a muddy bank and pulled the boat, with me still in it, halfway up the bank. I followed, but was less successful on the soft earth than my companion, stumbling twice before I stood erect on terra firma amongst herb-fragranced woodland.

Without words, we trudged through what became a heavy wood, until we reached a large, open clearing. As twilight turned to night, he lit a fire.

We sat gazing into the flames and I felt a little hungry. To my delight, my friendly friar produced a satchel from under his habit, and from it passed me bread, cured meat and wine. We shared this simple meal like it was some great banquet.

The food, wine and fresh air affected me. I was both merry and sleepy/ I stretched and yawned and for the first time I spoke to my companion, telling him I was ready for sleep. He looked me in the eye and though his lips did not move, he was speaking to me and I could hear him. His words were like velvet whispers and the sound of the night time forest disappeared as though I had attuned only to him. He asked me to look into the flames of the fire, and as I did so, I became hypnotised by the flickering flames and the glow of the embers. Amazingly, as I watched, an image came into focus. At first it was strange and unfamiliar, but as I continued to gaze, I could hear his voice gently narrating all that I saw.

As I looked at the vision of the night sky with more stars than I had ever seen, suddenly a white orb came into view, then it passed to reveal a beautiful blue, green, and white sphere that turned in the starry night. As I watched I felt such joy and then instantly saw a young man and a beautiful young woman dressed in clothes I had never seen before. The man kissed the woman gently, and lightly patted her stomach. She gazed down at his hand and then placed her hand over his and squeezed it. The voice then said, `Sleep now. Your mother is waiting`."

Alan finally opened his eyes and rubbed them energetically. He looked around to see everyone staring at him in complete awe. "What?" he asked, seemingly oblivious to the tremendously moving events that had just been recounted?

Jenny's Story

Soul Mates

Jenny, a lady in her early sixties came to see me at my studio in Bold Street, Liverpool, for a psychic reading.

As soon as she entered, a feeling of familiarity hit me. I just could not put my finger on why. The reason for this feeling of somehow knowing her was soon resolved.

"I came to one of your what-do-you-ma-call-it's - about other lives," she declared.

"Please do sit down and make yourself comfortable. I never forget a face," was my response, pointing her to a chair which had supported many a soul over the years. She launched into an explanation of the reason for her visit:

"I didn't get much out of it, though - well, not at first. Not until some weeks later. I was out for drive with a friend of mine - lovely man; on his own now; has been oh, seven or eight years. Anyway, as I was saying, he was taking us out for a drive; we do that - Southport, Chester, oh, all over the place. He's a smashing dancer, does all the old stuff, and disco too. Anyhow, we were going to Ormskirk Market but roadworks sent us off on some detour all round the houses, as they say, but there were no houses - if you know what I mean."

"Yes," I said. But before I could comment further, she continued.

"Well, we passed this old house just as we went over a little bridge, that's part of what's left of the Leeds/Liverpool canal, so Ronnie told me. Oh, and do you know, I felt like someone had walked over my grave. I just shuddered, and I could not get that house out of my mind," she paused and looked straight into my eyes. "What do you think?" she asked, holding my gaze.

I was about to respond, when she hurried on.

"Well, I'll tell you, that night I was out like a light. It must have been all the fresh air; my head hit the pillow and that was it, dead to the world. I overslept the next morning, even missed Kilroy as well! So once I was up, I made a cuppa and put Billy and Wally on the radio. Oh, they are funny; that 'Hold Your Plums'! I'm sure they put it on, acting like that. Hey, and it was you doing your stuff on dreams, and that was it. No wonder I overslept. I'd been dreaming all night. It all came to me; it must have been that house. I dreamt I was standing outside it just looking - I didn't go in. I just stood there and it was funny. I was watching it, well, watching it in my dream. Do you think that was a past life?" She paused. " I do."

She sat forward, resting her elbow on the desk between us.

"It's possible, but I'm not sure. I would need to know more. Has anything else happened, or have you had any more dreams about the house?" I tried to unravel the incident more precisely.

"Oh, yes. Lots of things, but that's not why I'm here. I want to know if I'm moving, because you see, Ronnie wants to move to Gibraltar, and wants me to go with him, so what do you think?"

"Fine," I smiled. "Here, shuffle these, if you would."

I passed her my tarot deck, took her date of birth, and proceeded with her reading. This actually threw up more than she had anticipated. I saw no move to Gibraltar for her, but surprisingly she was happy about this, as she hoped to persuade Ronnie to stay closer to home. They could then be happy together, without moving too far from her family.

"Thank you," she grinned. "Oh, you have put my mind at rest."

Jenny sat back, still smiling, and then began to gather herself ready to leave. Standing, she leaned forward again.

"I must tell you, in the dream I was a little girl and all scruffy. I know it was me. Anyway, I must dash. Ronnie will be waiting."

"Goodbye, and take care," I said, as I shook her hand.

"Oh, Tarra. Giz a hug!" she blurted out, embracing me on her whirlwind way out.

Once she left, I checked my watch and realised that I would miss my usual train home, and so I thought I would indulge myself with a cappuccino, and a slice of lemon meringue pie at Maggie May's Cafe.

I was just locking up, with the taste of sweet meringue and sharp lemon already in my mouth, when Jenny reappeared.

"Oh, I'm glad I've caught you before you go. Silly me! I want some of that pink crystal, and it slipped my mind because of all the talking we've been doing!"

So I opened up my office again, thinking to myself hungrily, 'There goes my lemon meringue!'

"This won't take long. I know the piece I want. I saw it as soon as I came in before. This is the one!" she announced.

She proceeded to pick out a piece of smooth rose quartz, the size of a small egg. It was kidney-shaped. One half was quite a clear rose, almost translucent; the other half rather milky in appearance.

"Are you sure?" I asked. "You should take your time in choosing the right one for you," I advised.

"I'm sure this is the one for me. How much is it?"

"That's okay. You're welcome to have it," I smiled.

"No. I couldn't. I must pay," she insisted, opening up her bag.

"No, really, it's okay. I'll tell you what. Why not come back at some time and tell me more about that dream. That will be recompense enough."

After thanking me enthusiastically. Jenny left.

Two weeks later, she was back, this time with Ronnie. We all made ourselves comfortable. I made sure of that as I had an inkling that this would be a lengthy session.

Jenny began her recollection after several chatty changes of subject.

"Remember how I was saying that I could see myself as a little girl?"

I nodded.

"Well, I saw a lot more than that. I saw her whole life. I say 'her' because even though I know it was me, I was watching it a bit like watching telly. I kind of saw the whole picture. You see after that first dream, I had few more recurring dreams. That's why I decided to try that technique you taught us, and you know, it works."

"Which of the techniques was that?" I asked with interest.

"The rose quartz one," she chirped.

"But you only just picked a piece a couple of weeks ago," I remarked.

"I know, but I still have my old one as well. I just wanted another piece for Ronnie," she explained.

"Sorry," I said. "Do continue."

She resumed.

"I could see Isabel! Isabel, that's her name, was standing outside the door of that very same house I saw out in the country. Isabel, no more than seven years old and holding the hand of a nun. Sister Asunta, who helped with the poor at an Infirmary just outside Prescot. Sister Asunta took her vows very seriously and considered herself a bride of Christ, living for her love of Jesus, with the utmost obedience to her order.

So this nun was happy in her daily duties of tending to the most helpless and pathetic wretches of God's children, knowing no limit to her compassion, and never reflecting on the futility of life. So immovable was her faith, so deep, that she was certain every soul would be saved from damnation, and bask in the glory of the Holy Trinity, and enter into Heaven.

Isabel stood with her hand in the gentle but firm grip of the kindest person she had ever known. She and Sister Asunta paused in front of the house. Isabel had never seen such a house. It reached all the way to the sky, and the brass knocker was polished to such a high degree that Isabel was sure she would be able to see her face in it.

Sister Asunta raised the bright knocker and rapped thrice on the door, in response to which the door opened and an arch of light flickered and sent rays through the stained glass window illuminating all around with a coat of arms depicting a triple chevron in red over a flaming sword pointing skywards. It had not yet turned to night but, nonetheless, the door and stained glass window dominated Isabel's view. She was afraid of what was beyond that door.

It seemed like the longest moment of the little girl's life, waiting for that door to open, she was reluctant to move from where she stood, with her hand clasped in the warmest, loveliest hand she had ever known.

The door opened and to Isabel's obvious relief the face that came from the other side was a friendly young woman who reminded her of - well, of kindness itself. 'Do come in' the kind-faced lady said. The nun stepped in with little Isabel at her side.

'Is the Magistrate himself in?' she asked.

'No'/ came the reply, 'but we are expecting the little miss.'

'Well, that's fine, then,' said Sister Asunta. She crouched down to Isabel. 'This is your new home now, Isabel, so you be a good girl, and I will come and see you soon. Off you go now.'

She kissed Isabel gently on each cheek, then let go of her hand, turned and was gone. Isabel took the kind lady's hand as it was offered and the door closed behind them, leaving Isabel on the brink of a new life.

Sister Asunta climbed aboard the horse trap, and headed back to the infirmary, completely satisfied with herself. She had found a wonderful home for Isabel, where she would not only be cared for and well-educated, but wanted and loved. The Magistrate was such a good and God-fearing man, whose compassion knew no bounds.

Isabel was led to the kitchen with her hand clasped in the lady's, who softly introduced herself as Anna. To Isabel it seemed that she was in a veritable palace, everything was so grand. In all honesty, it was a comfortable house, but all the same it was still just a house and not the palatial mansion Isabel thought she was in."

Jenny paused, drew a deep sigh, and smiled brightly before continuing.

"Isabel enjoyed the supper she had that evening. All she ate was a simple fish pie, with a drink of goat's milk, but it was the first time in her life she could remember eating enough and without others fighting over what was on her plate.

As the years passed, Isabel grew from the little fragile girl into a polite and well-mannered young woman. She was, however, not the young lady Sister Asunta had imagined. Her education was limited to that of a girl who was destined to go into service, not conducive to the life of a privileged young lady the nun had hoped and expected when she gave Isabel over the Magistrate. However, Isabel was happy enough and as good a Christian as one could hope, so Sister Asunta could hardly complain. On the contrary, she praised her guardian for his kind ways.

Isabel could not isolate the precise time when things changed. There was not one particular event or even some tragedy that occurred, but as with the nature of these things, slowly and inexorably change encompassed the house. Isabel seemed to experience the change from bright, endlessly sunny days where winter never seemed to figure, to a dark, cold house that never seemed warm enough, to then becoming a shabby and cold residence, where dust swarmed over everything no matter how hard Isabel worked. She did indeed find the work increasingly hard as, one by one, the indoor-staff left and were not replaced.

Isabel herself thought about leaving on several occasions, but she stayed, perhaps remembering the good days, and hoping that maybe they would return soon. She also felt a strong loyalty to the Magistrate, despite his reserve; or maybe it was that since the veil over her early life had been drawn, the house had become her only true home.

Isabel never wanted to lift the veil and remember her past, as she knew it was best left behind, rather like the rock that remains lifeless until it is lifted, releasing a multitude of small life.

Whichever way she looked at it, she was happy in her own lonely way. She loved to work. It filled her long, empty days. Mondays and Fridays were the better days, as provisions were delivered by Isaac then. She had seen him grow from a shy boy who was so quiet that Isabel assumed him to be mute. But over the years he had grown handsome and just a little bolder, and the few words that had passed between them became precious to her; she would spend days working out something, anything, to talk about. Sometimes she would even complain about the goods he would bring as it was all she could think of, even if the provisions were of the highest quality.

One Friday Isabel had taken extra care about her appearance. She always rose early, of course, but on Mondays and Fridays she completed all her duties quickly so that she had time to look her best. However, on this particular day, she had made an extra special effort. She decided to ask Isaac if he would like to stay a while and eat with her. The Magistrate had taken to long drinking sessions and would stay out late, especially on Fridays.

Isabel dressed herself in a simple cotton dress which buttoned up to the neck and reached down to her ankles, over which she donned a pristine white, bibbed apron. Her hair was freshly washed and tied back in a style which would make most women look austere, but in Isabel's case left her beauty undiminished. Her strawberry blonde hair balanced her fair freckled face, which, now in its early twenties, was full and round, with rosy cheeks, cupid bow lips, and lapis blue eyes; she was a sight to behold.

Had she but known it, Isabel did not need to make any special effort to impress, as Isaac already loved her and everything about her, though he did not have the courage to tell her. She was a dream to him, and he had learned early on in his disadvantaged life that his dreams never came true.

Isabel had stood for what seemed an eternity at an upstairs window watching the path from the high road which led to the village. From where this vantage point, she could see most of the houses, shops and the local Catholic church. The nearest building to the Magistrate's house was Ben's stables and smithy, where Ben, his wife and their large brood of nine children also lived. Ben seemed to be a kindly man, but Isabel had never really got to know him or his family particularly well; she was a bit of a loner really. As Isabel sat pondering on how making friends seemed never to happen easily, she was forced to ask herself, was it her own disposition, or had she become a timid mouse as the Magistrate turned gradually into an angry bear?

She had become afraid of her own shadow. Better to just get on with her chores and forget all about the outside world, she consoled herself. Then Isabel's heart leapt, her stomach fluttered and she held her breath as Isaac appeared from the smithy pushing his cart, now lighter as the provisions he was bringing to her were his last delivery of the day. Leaving the window, she hurried to the kitchen door and had opened it before Isaac arrived, so that when he entered, he would be met by the sight of her busy at the kitchen table.

'Good day. Miss Isabel,' said Isaac, wanting to enunciate the words clearly and positively in the way Ben had rehearsed with him, advising that only the courageous could win a maiden as fair as Isabel. But nerves got the better of him and instead he mumbled the words as usual, groaning inwardly. He need not have worried, for Isabel felt that he had the sweetest voice, even if spoken so quietly she had to strain to hear the words.

'And good day to you Master Isaac. Come along. Put those down on the table here/' she instructed.

She kept her head down as she spoke, her hands busy filling jars with preservatives. Despite it being uncomfortable, she strained her eyes so as to watch him as he moved closer. His face was flushed and shiny with a break out of sweat, and his long raven hair was untied, falling over most of his face, partially hiding his rich dark eyes.

His nose was longer than it should be, but nevertheless it was a proud nose that leaned slightly to the left, perhaps telling of a blow to it in the distant past, but making him look strong and capable. His lips were gentle and soft, matching the way he spoke, and how she wanted to feel when kissed.

'Sit you down, and I will fetch you an ale, cold from the pantry,' she gently bossed him.

Isaac sat down, wanting to continue a conversation, but the words he hoped for deserted him.

'There,' she smiled, placing down a tankard before him, foaming over the brim.

He intended to say thank you, but just stared at it; it looked like the finest tankard of ale he had ever seen. Putting both hands over it he lifted the brew to his lips and drank greedily, hoping the hops would restore his voice. He stopped gulping, then held the tankard up, looking at it with admiration, finally pronouncing in clear round words:

'That's truly a fine brew. Miss.'

'Isabel or Bel - don't call me Miss,' she smiled.

'Isabel, sorry, I just thought I should - you know - be respectful.'

'You are!' she beamed, inside and out. 'You are always respectful; the most respectful person I ever met,' she moved close to him and took his right hand in her own. 'I have prepared a rabbit stew for his worship, but there is plenty and I would love to have your company and for you to take supper with me,' she bit her lip nervously.

'Why, Miss, er sorry, Isabel, I truly would; thank you,' as he accepted the invitation he nodded his head in deference, out of habit which just made Isabel feel more deeply in love with this gentle man.

After supper, Isaac left with the confident stride of a man whose world was blooming. She had kissed him on the cheek, and that gentle touching on his face from her angelic lips would change his life for ever.

Isabel was back at the upstairs window watching Isaac push his now empty cart along the high road. Her heart was beating like never before, and all she could do was go over and over in her mind the kiss and how it made her feel; so weak and wobbly that she was sure her legs would give way.

Once he was out of her view she went to her room and lay on her bed trembling with so many emotions that she thought she would go mad or burst. Then she began to sob, she had lost all control and just excitedly sobbed until she was calm again.

The Magistrate was home as the light of day was fading. He never spoke other than to give orders or demand something. Thus Isabel was taken unawares that evening when he enquired if all was well with her/ as she served his supper.

'It's rabbit, sir/ was all she could think to say, as conversations were not part of the daily routine.

'I did not ask what it was, though I am sure it is fine fare you put before me. I ask if you are well.'

'Very well, I am very well, sir.'

She blurted the words out so quickly they sounded strained.

'Good, good. Leave me now.'

That night sleep came quickly for Isabel, but it was a sleep filled with dreams the whole night through. She dreamed about Sister Asunta, now at peace, but who until she died, had come to visit her every month. Her sixteenth birthday was the last time she had seen the kindly nun.

In Isabel's dream the nun was swimming in a beautiful clear lake and as she swam she beckoned her to join her, but in the dream, Isabel just stood on the bank of the lake and watched.

Then she dreamed of Anna who looked just as she had when Isabel had first come to the Magistrate's house, gentle and kind, holding her hand and feeding her fish pie. In the dream Anna was in a kitchen, a different kitchen from the one here at the house, but it felt familiar.

Anna was cooking and preparing food and as she did so she was talking all the time to Isabel, but in a language that she could not understand.

Then she had a dream which she had occasionally had before. It was a dark dream and reminded her of a time before she came to this house. In the dream she was a small child, little more than an infant, and she was on a longboat travelling slowly along a canal when she was startled by a splash of something or someone falling into the water. At that point she woke from her sleep, damp with sweat, as she had done so many times before from that same dream on a longboat. She knew there was more to remember, but she could not recall any more, no matter how hard she tried.

She washed her face, hoping the cold water would also clear her head, as all the previous night's dreams continued to swirl around her mind.

As she dressed, her thoughts turned to the good days at the house. This lifted her spirits and she smiled, then Isaac's face appeared in her head smiling, and the memory of their kiss warmed her, and all was well with the world. In this state of mind, even the Magistrate seemed a bit more human than he had been for many years.

The Magistrate, born Joshua Melchum, the third son of an untitled landowner, had not always been so stern. He had enjoyed a happy childhood and a good education in preparation for the law. He had once been a thoughtful and philanthropic young man, who had chosen a bachelor life and the company of other men over that of a happy family. He became a Magistrate at a young age, and so people originally called him 'the Magistrate' as a term of endearment and respect. Over the years his baptised name was forgotten.

He had earned a reputation for fairness, justice and wisdom; a God-fearing man who always acted in the spirit of the law. In his twenties and early thirties the Magistrate was a lean and handsome man who took great care over his appearance, often setting new sartorial standards. However, things changed. Without anyone knowing why, he began to drink excessively, putting on layers of fat with great ease. His handsome face became toughened, despite its round appearance, and the rosacea of his cheeks and nose contrasted strongly with the pallor of the rest of his skin.

The King's justice was now dispensed by the Magistrate without compassion and some even suggested, behind their hands, with a sadistic malice.

So from his middle to senior years, the high respect with which he was once held, turned inevitably to fear. People would speculate about this change; without any proof, they assumed that the Magistrate's dear and close friend, Sebastian Hoole, was the cause of the dramatic transformation that occurred. He left the Magistrate for Venice, never to return, leaving his friend a somewhat saddened and embittered man.

A few mornings later, Isabel was about her duties as usual. She had built a fire in the Magistrate's living room and the kitchen as, despite being summer, a cold wind had brought heavy rain. This inclement weather could not suppress her joy at the day ahead and she prepared his worship's breakfast with unprecedented enthusiasm. The oatmeal was smooth and creamy with a little extra sugar, spice and honey. She was about to serve this perfect porridge, accompanied with warmed cider, in the dining room, as was his wont, when she was stopped in her tracks by his sudden and unexpected appearance in the kitchen. He had never ventured into her domain before.

'Isabel!' he cheerfully bawled. 'I want to talk to you, and it is better done here. Ah, yes, I have a great appetite today. Please put the breakfast down here.' He smiled broadly and pointed to the kitchen table. Isabel stood still, momentarily bewildered by the unusual request, and the happy disposition of a man of whom she had become afraid. The Magistrate, now settled at the table, urged her:

'Come, woman, am I to eat or watch the oatmeal grow cold?'

'Sorry, sorry sir!" she stuttered, as she mentally shook herself, and placed the tray on the table.

'Sit down, Isabel.'

She did not have to be told again, as despite this out-of-character bonhomie she still felt the cold finger of fear around him.

'Why, you are all a shiver, woman,' he observed. 'Are you cold, or unwell; what ails you?'

'No, sir. I am well,' she answered, gathering her composure.

'Good. I have good and happy news for you. I know I am not the easiest man in the world. This house - I wonder sometimes whether it is a home or a prison for you. I have been so wrapped up in myself I have had no time to look at what is happening around me in this house. It seems barely yesterday that this was a busy, lively and good home. Now I see it is but a pale shadow of what it once was.'

He paused to watch for her reaction, but she continued to sit listening to him, with her eyes glazed over as though his words were just washing over her.

'Isabel, I have given a great deal of thought to you and your situation here, and I think, no, I am sure, the company of another person would be just the thing you need.'

'Company, sir?' she enquired, not knowing what he really meant by the vague offer.

'Yes, lass, company. I think it is high time you be courted and wed. What do you think?'

There was a silence so palpable it could have been sliced with a knife.

'Well, speak up. Is it not time to think about what you want - a husband, a good man for you?'

'I don't know, sir,' she stammered uncomfortably.

'You don't know, lass?' he echoed.

'No, sir.'

'Oh, it matters not what you know. I know a good man who is looking for a wife, and when I spoke of you to him he was delighted. He will be here this very day.'

This information hit Isabel as though someone had actually given her a blow to her solar plexus. She knew there could only be one man for her, and that was Isaac.

Quickly, she responded.

'No, I do not think it is yet time for a husband,' she said emphatically.

'Come, come, lass. I know you will be pleased at your good fortune when Mr. Hardacre walks into your life.'

Isabel's head was so full of thoughts rushing around that she became quite dizzy; she felt her temperature rise and a sweat break out on her forehead and before she knew it she had swooned into an involuntary faint. The Magistrate lifted Isabel's head and lightly slapped her face. Her eyes flickered back into focus to see his concerned face looking back at her.

'Dear me. You are all a flutter,' he smiled, as he helped her to a seat and placed a reassuring hand on her shoulder. 'Don't fret so. Once you have seen what I have arranged for you, you will have good reason to faint!' He spoke to Isabel as a doting father would to a favourite daughter.

He had calculated that she was overcome with excitement at the prospect of marriage. He was so wrong. Isabel was in a panic. How could she escape this situation? She had nowhere else to go if she ran away, no means of supporting herself and Isaac. She loved him so much, but would he be able to take her, how could he? He was also penniless. These thoughts and many more raced around her head, until the anxiety caused tears to course uncontrollably from so deep inside her she thought she would cry forever.

The Magistrate spent the rest of the day smiling to himself as he organised his affairs. He wrote several letters. What he had not yet told Isabel was none of her business, but would have a great affect on her life. He had been a good and conscientious guardian, and given her a far better life than she could have hoped for. With her now soon to be married, he felt justified in all he had done and now it was time for him to go and find happiness himself - a happiness he felt was long overdue and was to be found in Geneva. He had read and re-read the letter from his old friend asking, pleading rather, for him to join him in Switzerland. So everything was to be sold up and a new life beckoned for the Magistrate too.

Isabel was oblivious to what was happening and how quickly it would all come to pass. She only knew she was expected to marry a man she did not know or love. How could this ever possibly happen when she was deeply in love with Isaac? A desperate plan began to hatch in her mind, a plan inconceivable and without any possible hope of success.

Frantic, she decided she would visit Old Peggy, a local wise woman and midwife, to purchase a sleeping draught with which she would lace the Magistrate's midday meal in the hope that he would sleep the day and night through. In this way she hoped to make it look as though there was not a soul home when Mr Hardcastle called, thus giving her time to speak to Isaac. Surely he loved her? They could elope; they would be wed no matter what.

With all of these tumultuous thoughts crowding her mind, she set off to

Old Peggy's derelict house, a good hour's walk from the village in a copse off the northern road.

Before Isabel had worked out what she actually wanted, or what to say, she was knocking at the door. It was opened by a small, emaciated old figure who looked at her with surprisingly bright and piercing eyes of such a dark brown that it was practically impossible to distinguish the pupil; the whole appearance was of two burning coals staring deep into her very soul.

Isabel was momentarily afraid, regretting her swift decision to visit this old crone, when the woman invited her across the threshold with a hoarse whisper, leaving the girl with no time to ponder further on the rashness of her behaviour.

Isabel nervously did as she was bid, and followed the old woman into the one room, which was surprisingly clean, bright and well-furnished, not at all what she had expected to find, judging from the dilapidated exterior of the building.

'Thee be Melcham's demirep. Is thee carrying a child?' she croaked.

The old crone's ancient turn of phrase disturbed Isabel.

'No!' Isabel shouted emphatically, and then 'No!' again.

The old woman took a seat and said, 'I don't get folk calling just to pass a word, so thee must be in some sort of trouble and wanting help. Speak up, what's tha want?' she barked.

Isabel said nothing, she had come with a half-baked idea and now felt foolish.

'Sit thee down, and then maybe words will happen.'

Isabel accepted the proffered chair, 'Thank you ma'am. I have come to you with reason enough, but now, well, I don't know.'

Within minutes, Isabel emptied her heart to Peggy and nothing was left out. Within the hour Isabel was on her way back with dried mushrooms to make a drinking broth.

'Give him the brew and the Magistrate will sleep both day and night, maybe even the next day, and be none the worse - maybe even better for it/' the old crone had advised.

Once back at the house, Isabel began to prepare the midday meal when she heard a horse and rider approach the house. By the time she had reached the door, the Magistrate was already greeting the stranger. Her heart sank. She had not thought Mr Hardacre would arrive at such an early hour.

The Magistrate had noticed Isabel at the window. Speaking to William Hardacre, he said, 'You see, William, is she not a sweet, lovely thing?'

'I did not doubt your word, sir. You are a lucky man to have such a beauty under your roof, alone, just the two of you,' he smirked.

The Magistrate bridled as he felt an accusation in the barbed comment.

'I'm a man of honour, and see Isabel as a sweet child in my charge and have always treated her well, and never has such an occasion of her honour being compromised occurred.'

The Magistrate was visibly angry at the need to defend Isabel.

'No offence was meant, and I beg your pardon, but she is a handsome lass, is there lusty youth hereabout to tempt her favour?' William grinned on through crooked teeth.

For the first time the Magistrate examined his friend in an objective manner to see what a woman might look for. He was tall and muscular, a fine figure of a man, but not handsome and perhaps further along the road to middle age than was ideal for Isabel. Also his nature was not so kind as he had let himself be led to believe. However, the Magistrate dismissed these thoughts. He wanted to be free of any responsibilities, to sell his home and leave to make a new life in a new country.

Isabel was back in the kitchen after the midday meal of cold meat, cheese and bread. She managed to avoid eye contact with the man she had been instructed to marry. She had made excuses to avoid being drawn into any conversations, but said she would speak once her chores were done after supper. Whilst she was busy cooking mutton and vegetables she came to the conclusion that she would have to send both men to sleep, then she could make her escape from this nightmare that had suddenly taken over her life. Without really thinking - her actions were automatic - she emptied all the dried mushrooms into the stew pot and set it to cook slowly. As an afterthought she added a half bottle of brandy, just to ensure a deep sleep.

Isabel then did something else she had never done before. She left the house and went to look for Isaac; he had to know how she felt about him. She headed first for the smithy, not really expecting to find him there, but thankfully he was.

Isaac was helping the blacksmith at the forge. As soon as he saw her, Isaac put down the iron tongs and hammer. He knew something must be amiss by the simple fact she was standing there before him.

'What's happened? Is there some ill, that you are here?' Isaac spoke clearly as he asked the questions with evident concern.

Isabel was surprised and pleased at his bold and incisive enquiry.

'No, Isaac, I just wish a word with you, if you would be so kind.'

'Yes, it is no penance to me. Miss er, I mean Isabel.' They both looked at Ben.

'Don't fret for me. I need to see to the mare in foal.'

The smithy winked and left.

Isabel wasted no time getting to the point.

'Dear Isaac, I have only a few moments to speak with you on a matter of grave importance.'

'What be the matter?' he asked with earnest concern.

'Have you ever looked upon me as a wife, thought of a life for us together?' she asked boldly.

As she said the words she watched his eyes, hoping to see no sign of doubt. There was none. She sighed deeply.

Isaac had not taken in the fullness of the question. He had not realised what she was asking of him, nonetheless his answer gladdened and filled Isabel's heart with joy.

'I think of nothing else, but never did I hope such thoughts ever to come true.'

'Would you elope with me, this very moment if I begged such a thing of you?' she rushed.

'Without any reserve I would run away with you if it could be, and not some dream.'

'It is no dream, for I am desperate,' her voice broke with insuppressible panic.

Isaac looked into her eyes and saw something he did not fully understand. She was truly sad over some great trouble. He began to realise that this was not some teasing game she was playing, it was real and something he did not know about was grievously amiss.

'Come to the house at the turn of dark and bring two horses. Now I must away.' She began to scuttle quickly from the smithy, then turned back to Isaac: 'You can do this. I have put my hope in you.'

Then she was gone, leaving Isaac stunned by such a random and urgent revelation. He would of course do anything for Isabel, but he had no horse, let alone two, and little money. Ben returned to the forge to be confronted by a stupefied and happy Isaac.

'She is a fine lass, the prettiest I've laid eyes on,' said Ben when told the news. ''Tis a pity she speaks so loud, all the village may have heard what passed between you.' Isaac did not answer his friend and mentor. 'Methinks you love her and would do all she bids.'

'Yes I would, but how can I? I have nothing to give her, yet. I must do as she asks, she seemed so ...' he did not finish what he was to say as his thoughts leapt wildly in every direction.

'You must be there, as she asked,' Ben reasoned.

'How?'

Ben shrugged his shoulders and opened his hands to Isaac's question.

'I dare not ask further.'

'No, that would be unwise.'

'Could I take two horses from you? I would return them once we were safely placed somewhere,' Isaac tried.

Ben scratched his head and then started the forge furnace, 'Come on, I have work to do and need your help lad'.

Isaac could not understand Ben's attitude. In the past he had always been encouraged by him to follow his heart where Isabel was concerned.

'I am sorry, but I cannot think on this job whilst I worry so for Isabel.'

'Well you had better think on it lad, I want this work done if you are to be gone this night and me to be left with no strong arms to help me, or two of my best horses, and I suppose silver to put in your pocket,' he smiled.

'Ben, what are you saying, do you mean ...?' the boy could not believe his ears.

'Aye, lad, you take two fine beasts for you and Isabel, and go with my best wishes and purse of silver too.'

Meanwhile, back at the Magistrate's, the mutton stew with its extra potency was served from a tureen to the two unsuspecting diners who had already drunk wine with enthusiasm, and were ready for a good helping of meat to be washed down with more Burgundy. Isabel was relieved that little attention had been shown to her, and the Magistrate had ordered her out and not to disturb them until he called for her.

Isabel dallied in the kitchen, not knowing how long it would take for the potion to work, not knowing whether it would work or what effect it would have should it do so. What was only minutes seemed like hours as she anxiously waited; then her waiting was over.

The kitchen door burst open. William Hardacre staggered through, swaying as he made his way towards her. His eyes were bloodshot and his lip was bleeding profusely; he reached out with a hand and clutched his stomach with the other. Before he had taken another step he sank to his knees, falling forward and heavily hitting his face on the kitchen table.

Isabel instinctively ran to him, but it was too late. He was giving up his last breath. She touched his face, now bloody and disfigured, the contact causing nausea to rise up within her. She recoiled in shock from the now lifeless body of Mr Hardacre.

'Jesus, Mary and Joseph!' she screamed, crossing herself frantically. 'What have I done?!' she choked.

She put her hand to her mouth in a desperate attempt to silence herself.

She gathered herself and ran to the dining room to find the Magistrate was not there.

'Sir!' she yelped.

She called out several times, then ran into the hall. She stopped in her tracks as she saw the Magistrate at the top of the stairs.

'Sir! Are you well?" she asked, hoping against hope that he was without harm.

The Magistrate seemed not to hear her, but simply stared blankly, his eyes fixed upon some unseen thing. He stepped forward, missing his footing as he did so, and tumbled down the stairs headfirst.

The sickening crack of his neck breaking as he smacked into the floor at the foot of the stairs, caused Isabel to shudder, and she fell to the ground moaning.

'No, no, it cannot be. What is this?' she murmured through heavy tears.

Slowly she reached out and tentatively touched the Magistrate. There was no movement at all. He appeared to be stone dead.

She found she was unable to move herself; she was transfixed, trapped in eye-to-eye contact with the corpse's unseeing stare, the glassy eyes wide open in the head set at an impossible angle to his body. She would have stayed locked in this catatonic state for perhaps eternity, were it not for the sound of Isaac's voice calling her name.

'Here, I am here, in the hall!' she shrieked, piercing the atmosphere so heavy with anguish.

Isaac, at the sound of her voice, ran to her. He had already seen the body of a stranger seeping blood onto the kitchen floor. What he saw in the hall was even worse - a grim, ugly corpse of a man he knew well and was afraid of.

'What devilry, mischief, has been done, and by who?! Are you hurt?'

His questions poured out in torrent of disbelief. Then he gathered himself and lifted her and held her close. Gripping him tightly she broke into floods of tears that shook her entire body. Isaac held her for some minutes, then stepped back, but continued holding her in strong arms as he held her out to look into her face.

'Are you harmed?' he asked softly. There was a fear of the unknown in his voice. 'Isabel. Did they hurt you?'

She looked at him and then shook her head.

'Who did this?' he pleaded desperately.

She closed her eyes, then moved towards him again so that he could once again encircle her in his comforting hug.

Isaac held her at his breast. Then a thought occurred to him. The perpetrator could still be here, or could it be the stranger who lay dead already? he wondered in a daze.

'How many were there? Who would do such a thing? I must away and get some help,' he panicked. He was thinking aloud, rather than talking to Isabel.

'No!' she whispered desperately.

'But I must. Some brigands are about, and I will not be long,' he tried again.

'No! No! You don't understand. It is all my fault, everything that happened here.'

'What are you saying? Isabel! What ...?' he stopped.

'I did it! I did what you see - but I did not mean to do such harm!'

Isaac's face fell, 'No, it is not so! You could not slay two men! It's not true!' he cried.

'But it is true! It was my hand that acted against them both, but I did not intend that they should die.'

'Shush, shush. Do not speak such words. Do not mock me, when men lie dead at the hands of another.'

'I do not mock. I wish it was so, but I am the one who did this, no other hand ...' She stopped before she finished what she intended to say, and then chastised herself: 'Foolish bitch! I am a foolish woman!'

'What?' demanded the bewildered boy.

'Isaac, please believe me! It is my fault what happened here, but it was not my hand alone!'

'I cannot understand!' he tremored.

'Nor do I - but now I must pay the price!' her tears re-emerged.

'What do you mean, I do not understand?' Isaac shook her.

'I will start at the beginning.'

The two stood facing each other, just inches away from the Magistrate's corpse, as Isabel explained all that had happened that day - the visit to Old Peggy, the mushrooms she put in the stew, how she had meant to send them to sleep, so that she and Isaac could elope.

'The potion was bad; it poisoned them, sent them delirious, and they both died by mishap because of its effect on them,' she offered. She sighed as she finished her account of the day.

'We must go, and go now quickly, to be far away, before all is discovered,' Isaac exclaimed.

'No, Isaac. We cannot, we would be caught and you would be blamed also for helping me,' she choked.

'No, you cannot stay. You would be hanged as a murderess or a witch. You cannot stay. I still have the horses ready outside, and silver. Let us be away!'

Eventually, Isabel agreed there was no choice but to flee. Her heart was broken. She had thought she would be eloping with her love to live in happiness for ever; this was now an impossible dream. They were to flee, fugitives, to maybe be brought back at any time to be judged for a crime which, no matter how unintentional, would still be her responsibility.

And so it was that Isaac, that night, buried both bodies and made the house clean and in the best order he could. They set off together before daybreak, riding north, not quite sure of where they would go, only aware of the great distance that needed to be covered.

As the sun came up, and having travelled only a little way, they were stopped by Old Peggy. She was leaning on a staff in the middle of the highway.

'We have no time for your nonsense, old woman,' Isaac shouted at her.

'No, I must speak with her, grunted the old woman. Isabel touched Isaac's arm before dismounting.

'Are they dead?' Peggy asked the question seeming already to know the answer.

'What did you do? You tricked me! You gave me an evil and deadly potion, and I used it in all innocence!' scowled Isabel.

'But are you not free?' asked the old woman, her eyes glistening.

'I need not have killed to be free. I just asked for your help to give the Magistrate a long sleep,' explained the girl.

'Well, he's got that now! Ha, ha, ha. He's got all the sleep he needs. Ha, ha, ha.' Peggy's tone turned venomous. 'And the other bastard. Is he dead too?'

'Did you know about him coming last evening?' asked Isabel, amazed.

'Yes, I knew,' came the reply.

'Why?'

'It's best you do not know,' she replied mysteriously.

'You cannot make me the hand of death and not let me know why,' demanded Isabel.

'You have no guilt; you knew not what was in the potion,' was the response.

'And when I am dragged to the gallows, will I have no guilt then?' asked Isabel bitterly.

'I wish I could be so sure,' Isaac interjected.

'Silence, fool!' hissed Peggy.

'I have waited here for you to pass, so I may give you this.' Peggy handed a simple gold band to Isabel. 'Wear this on your wedding finger, and you will be safe enough,' she announced.

Isabel did as she was bid without thanking the old woman, then asked again, 'Why? What reason, or was it mischief? Why should they have to die?'

'As I told you, you are best without knowledge. There is an order in nature and life, I have just restored that. Now go, go first north, then east, only settle when you pass Durham.'

'Come,' urged Isaac.

'Go, follow your fool. No harm will come if you do as I say. Settle in the north and east and say nothing of these parts. I will make all well here, now go, and live with him as man and wife, but do not lie with him or any man, stay pure and you will be safe from the laws of man,' she warned.

'What are you saying? I love Isaac. He is a good man and no fool, I cannot do as you say,' Isabel protested.

'Please yourself. I have warned you,' were the old woman's final words.

Isabel and Isaac eventually did settle in the Borders, where Isaac worked as a farrier and Isabel a cook at a manor house. Despite a lingering anxiety, their troubles did not catch up with them. They lived happily, and in love, but never once did they consummate their union.

Pneumonia took Isaac in his forty-ninth year, and Isabel lived on for a further three years, later dying peacefully in her sleep."

Jenny paused for a moment, then opened her eyes.

"It was after Isabel died that she met Isaac again in the spirit world and a wonderful happiness was experienced, a beautiful heavenly life so full of love."

"Why did you come back?" I asked, curious to understand all that had happened.

"That I do not really know; no one knows all the whys. I can't remember, no matter how hard I try, what Heaven was like. All I have is an impression of happiness, great joy and love, but no memory at all of the place."

"Why do you call it 'Heaven'; I mean the place you were in, in spirit?" I asked.

"Just take it from me, it was," she stated with a contentment born of certainty.

"Then I accept your judgement."

"I knew when I met Ronnie there was something more than love there; a bond beyond the ordinary; we are soul-mates, in love and in past lives. We came together late in life, perhaps we should have met earlier," she smiled sadly.

I reassured her, "I believe it was meant to work out the way it has. Perhaps yours or Ronnie's karma needed to be balanced before you were to be together in love, as one."

"Well we were that all right, and enjoying every minute too."

Jenny and Ronnie subsequently married and now live in North Wales, still very much in love.

Darragh's Story

Egyptian Sands of Time

It was a cold February Saturday when I first met Darragh. I was walking around a Mind, Body and Spirit exhibition at the Bluecoat Chambers in Liverpool.

Stella, an ebullient and vivacious young woman, dressed in a somewhat out of place power suit, could be heard, before she was seen over the background music of medieval canticles. I was about to turn and retrace my steps when her loud voice peeled out,

"Darling!"

She ran over to me and loudly repeated, "Darling!" followed by a pair of air kisses to each side of my face. She confidently linked her arm through mine and began to march me to her exhibit stand for Aloe Vera.

"Raymond, you must come and meet my friend, Darragh. He is just wonderful, amazing. You just have to talk to him," she chirped.

We arrived at the Aloe Vera stand, fully stocked with the wonder potion, together with numerous posters and leaflets full of glowing testimonials, and scientific legends, pinned up on baize screens.

"Darragh, this is Raymond. Raymond this is Darragh," she introduced us.

He held out his hand, which I took and was surprised by the strength of his grip. He stood a little under six foot in height, and seemed impossibly thin, with a deep, nut-brown tan, bright blue eyes and a broad smile which showed off two rows of perfect white teeth. His salt and pepper hair, flanked at each temple with silver, was brushed back, exposing a perfectly symmetrical widow's peak.

He was incredibly well dressed. His grey suit was a perfect fit and had the look of being hand tailored. He wore a smart, blue, Oxford shirt with ample room at the neck, and he wore a burgundy silk tie with a matching pocket kerchief. This dapper man stood in highly polished ox-blood leather 'Comos'.

"Pleased to meet you," he said, with a voice soft and clear, with a hint of Irish brogue.

"And you," I responded sincerely.

"Darragh is a hypnotherapist, and also counsels at the University," enthused Stella.

"How interesting," I said, hoping I sounded so.

"So it is, that's why I brought you over to meet him. He's interested in past lives as well and I told him all about what you do," explained Stella.

"Yes, I was wondering if I could observe a regression session, at your convenience, and with the participant's agreement, of course," Darragh asked.

"By all means," I offered.

So it was that we exchanged business cards. I clutched his card in my hand as I made my excuses and left. I was putting it in my wallet when I read it, and to my surprise the card said: Father Darragh O'Rourke, Th.D; MBAH. A priest! This was a turn up for the books. I returned to Stella and asked her more about this sartorial priest, who also practised hypnotherapy and was interested in the field of natural therapies.

I was impressed to learn that not only was he a counsellor and therapist, he also practised Reiki and had opened a healing centre in North Wales, which to my surprise had the support of his order. In return, he helped the church understand the growth in New Age spirituality.

Some weeks passed before I heard from the priest. However, it transpired that his request was not simply to observe, but to help him to look at his own past lives. We made arrangements to carry out the regression the following week.

When Darragh arrived he was dressed immaculately once again in suit, collar and tie, with no hint of his priesthood. We spoke for some while before we began the regression. I discovered that this man was multi-faceted and had entered the priesthood at an early age, but in his mid-thirties had gone to India with voluntary services overseas. It was there that he had become interested in alternative medicine, guided also by a Spanish friar.

On his return to the UK he had studied psychology and subsequently become a counsellor. In addition, he had studied and started practising as many natural therapies as he could.

Not surprisingly, Darragh entered trance quickly and easily. We had agreed in advance that he would control his own regression. This was possible as he was a practising hypnotherapist and had a good understanding of the trance state.

Darragh's breathing had become deeper, his eyes were in REM, but no sound whatsoever emitted from his mouth. We had set a post-hypnotic suggestion in place, so Darragh would automatically describe what he was seeing. That he was observing something was obvious from his facial expressions and eye movements. The anticipation was punctuated by the sound of the tape recording machine clicking off.

Darragh blinked his eyes open.

"What ...?" he blurted out, seeming startled into consciousness by the noise of the cassette.

"It's nothing," I explained. "Just this switching off," I said pointing to the cassette recorder.

"Well, let's get started then." He sounded impatient.

"I beg your pardon!" I responded, puzzled by this remark. "What do you mean?"

"Have I missed something? I had just closed my eyes and started to drift when that machine clicked and woke me from my doze," he snapped.

"No, no," I disagreed. "That was forty-five minutes ago," I corrected him.

"Oh, you mean I fell asleep, not just dozed for a few seconds?" he seemed surprised.

"No, I don't think you were just asleep. I think you went into a trance," I responded.

"Oh, no. It is total amnesia. I must have gone very deeply into trance and then the noise of the cassette broke it, and shut the door to the past as well," Darragh sighed, sounding very disappointed.

We realised the solution to this problem was for Darragh to try and constantly commentate before, as well as whilst, he was in the regressive trance, as this would help to re-create the atmosphere of the past, and would more than likely eliminate any amnesia.

Darragh closed his eyes once again, and began to breathe deeply and slowly. He began:

"I can see a mirror. It is opaque, but shimmering, as if the reflection is under water. I am walking towards the mirror. I am reaching out with my hand to touch the surface, but it's not a hard surface or a reflection, it feels warm, no, hot. Sand; all I can see is sand for miles in every direction. I am no longer looking into the mirror. I am standing in a desert, and all I can see above me is a cloudless blue sky with a low sun and the sand everywhere.

Mat'tan. I am Mat'tan. My feet are small. I mean smaller than they should be. I feel strange, smaller than ...oh, no! " Darragh fell silent and shook his head, then sprung open his eyes.

"I don't think I should continue," he warned seriously.

"What's wrong?" I asked, a bit concerned.

"If I had not experienced it, I would not believe it possible," he stated.

"I'm sorry, Darragh, but I have no idea what you are talking about," I said, perplexed by his attitude.

"No. You haven't, have you?" he said with semi-amusement.

"I'll just wait then till you are ready to continue," I offered.

"I just did not expect what happened to happen. I was a woman!" he said, sounding completely astonished. "Analyse that, why don't you?!" he chided himself. "My goodness, that was such a shock, although I do know that we can be a different sex in past lives, as experiences during each life allow us to understand every facet of humanity, and thereby allow our soul to progress."

"Do you want to continue?" I asked.

"Yes. I'm okay now. As I said, it just shook me for a moment," he assured me.

Darragh again closed his eyes and within seconds I could see them moving under the lids as he was returning to the desert sands and cloudless blue sky.

"I am Mat'tan. It is the time of prayer. Soon night will fall. I must be on my way. As I turn to go back to the Necropolis there are many other people also out in the desert. I, like them, have been in the desert to talk to those who have already travelled into the West and live in the land of the Afterlife.

This is Egypt. It is the Time of the Hyena, and many are dead from the wars in the North, and the pharaoh is also dead. The Necropolis has never been so hectic. I work every day, and have done so all this season. I am with my husband. He, like me, is dressed in simple white linen. He is bald, as am I. Everyone else seems the same except some people wear wigs. You can tell those from the East side of the Nile in their fine clothes, oiled wigs and perfume. They come to visit their loved ones who have now travelled into the West, but left their bodies in palaces, mansion houses, mastabas, cooler and grander than my home.

I should not complain. My husband is a stonemason and is paid well; we eat meat every day, and I am in good health, as is my husband. Our only sorrow is that we have not yet been blessed with children.

We live in the Southern quarter of the Necropolis far enough away from the mortuaries not to breathe the air from the house of death. Our house is on three floors; the first for goats and geese; the second we use to bathe and avoid the heat of the day; the third is open to the sky and we live and sleep there mainly.

I have been happy in my life up to now, but my worry is my husband, Suni, who is a master mason, and has just been conscripted by the lord mason to work on the far away temple of our recently deceased pharaoh. There are rumours from the old days of masons never returning after working on the temple of the Lord Tuthmoses, and now that his son, Tuthmoses II, is dead, I fear my husband will not return."

Darragh suddenly blinked his eyes open.

"I don't believe it. I mean, it is inconceivable, almost fantastical. I feel everything, the smells, the noise, the emotions. Yes, I feel all her emotions ..." he mused.

He paused, then looked to me, "Do you come across false memory often whilst researching past-life regressions?"

"Yes, I do," I replied. "But over the years I have learned to spot the difference, and so far what you have described and the manner in which you have reported it would lead me to think this is not what is happening to you," I genuinely reassured him.

"Yes, quite, however it gives me problems because I am aware of her life, her feelings, her beliefs. It becomes unnerving for me. Yes, I am very open minded, and liberal for a Jesuit, but nonetheless I am a priest, and must contemplate a while on all I have experienced here."

Darragh then took his leave.

Two weeks passed before Darragh returned to continue his fascinating regression. Once again he made himself comfortable and relaxed, and only moments had passed when he began to speak.

"I am Mat'tan. It is dark tonight. There is no moon and I feel cold. This is not a very happy time. My Suni has been away now for such a long time. The Nile has flooded twice since we last spoke. I know something is wrong. Hafan, another master mason, has returned to his family on three occasions since Suni left, but he tells me he has not seen or heard anything of him."

Darragh's expression changed to a frown of consternation.

"This is strange," he complained, before pausing. Some minutes passed without him speaking further, so I decided to prompt him with questions.

"Darragh can you hear me?" I urged.

"Oh, yes, of course I can!"

He replied so easily, my first thought was that he had come out of trance, but had kept his eyes closed.

"You said something was strange?" I enquired.

"Yes, that's right. Suddenly the situation changed. I am no longer her, or I should say not inside Mat'tan. I am with her though. I am beside her, well not really. I am around her, that's the best way I can explain it. Above, in front and at her side all at the same time, quite unnerving at first. It made me feel a little nervous, but that has passed.

She is sitting as a passenger in a rowing barge which is moored at a quayside. It is so busy, there are hundreds of people. It absolutely stinks! But it is fantastic, with dogs and cats everywhere. She leaves the barge via a wooden gangway onto a platform with steps going in every direction. As she looks around I also see the large war barges being loaded with soldiers and provisions, and other barges are being loaded with livestock. She climbs the central steps which lead to the market. I am astounded by the variety of produce on display. What a rich life the Egyptians have.

She enters a small, single-storey stone building which has a red circle over the doorway. Two guards stand to attention at either side of the door-posts, dressed in white pleated kilts with a red belt supporting a sheathed sword.

Their chests are bare, but across their backs are slung a bow and a quiver of arrows. On both arms they wear red wrist lets and on their feet are red leather knee-length boots.

Inside she receives a pass to enter the House of a Thousand Years, the residence of the lord mason who is the permanent house guest of the new pharaoh, a boy king, although people say the real power lies with his half-sister, and it is only a matter of time before she will seize power from him

Mat'tan walked through the crowded streets that are nevertheless so clean it is a surprise to me. There are street cleaners and no sign of sewage problems despite the heat. Maybe these ancient people had more sophistication than we give them credit for.

She is entering a beer and cook-house which is thronged with priests and students from the House of Books, and temple hand-maidens enjoying the attention of the students.

Mat'tan is greeted warmly by a large, middle-aged man; it is her sister's husband. Soon her sister, Hanni, is also embracing her. Both women cry with joy as many years have passed since they last saw each other.

Mat'tan enjoys a cold beer and nibbles a little dried goose as she tells her sister her news and how she was about to have an audience with Seni at the House of a Thousand Years. Her sister feels afraid for Mat'tan and urges her to return after she has spoken with the lord mason, to stay with her until Suni was safely home. Hanni does not believe he will return, but keeps this thought to herself."

Peter suddenly paused, before continuing,

"A little time then passed. Mat'tan made her way to the House of a Thousand Years, with the help of Shufi, her teenage nephew who knew the city like the back of his hand. When she arrived at the palace, the house of the pharaoh, she could not believe her eyes. It was totally majestic. The walls on each side of the enormous cedar doors ran as far as the eye could see. The stone was a rose yellow, and carving depicting great deeds and battles of the pharaoh shone in brilliant colours along the length of the other walls. The door itself was also carved with lotus blossoms embossed with turquoise, lapis lazuli and gold. Three palace guards stood motionless in white kilts and white helmets. Each held a long spear.

Visitors from the countryside and other towns milled about in awe and wonder at the beauty of the palace. There were even artists who offered to sketch visitors to the pharaoh's House of a Thousand Years as a souvenir of their visit, as well as relic sellers who sold statues of the gods. This year's big sellers were Isis and Seth.

Mat'tan presented her pass to one of the guards, but he just ignored her. She tried with all of them but the response was the same. Then her nephew suggested trying one of the smaller gates, and reluctantly Mat'tan followed him. They found a small postern gate open and a queue of several people all holding papyrus documents just like the pass Mat'tan held. This was obviously the right gate. Mat'tan entered into a large, open garden with three pools, where both adults and children were bathing and enjoying the water.

She had been told to wait, so she did, taking in the scenery of this beautiful place. She had waited some time and now the sun was losing its ferocity. Then, just as her patience was giving out, a priest came over to greet her, and invited her to follow him.

Mat'tan was led along colonnades all covered in colourful pictures of life in Egypt, then she came to a long, sparse room without any furniture except for one large chair made entirely of gold. All the walls were of a white marble with veins that looked like polished silver. The floor was a sparkling blue and gold-speckled lapis lazuli. No gods were represented in this room at all; there were neither pictures nor statues.

This unusual room was cool despite there being no windows and it was as bright as day though no lamps were to be seen.

The priest left after telling Mat'tan to wait where she was. After waiting only a short time her nerves began to get the better of her. She felt very uncomfortable and afraid, and her need to relieve herself was becoming strong. She jumped with fear as she heard the slap of sandal on floor getting louder, but she could not tell from which direction. Suddenly she froze as the sound abruptly stopped. She could not see, but sensed the presence of someone in the room with her. Then a hand touched her shoulder from behind. She screamed out.

'Tu, tu,' the sound came echoing around the room, then two arms spun her around again.

'Tu, tu, what ails you so?'

The man's voice was deep, with a working class accent.

'What is it you want of me? I am a busy man in the work of the pharaoh.'

He spoke the words teasingly with a grin.

Mat'tan felt mocked, but was afraid to challenge this man, a lord in the house of pharaoh. She watched him before she answered.

He was tall, more than six foot, with a rugged, pock-marked face that was muscular. Even though his clothes were of the finest cloth, his hands were rough and dirty at the finger nails.

'You are the Lord Seni, the lord mason?' she asked with some trepidation.

'I am.'

'My husband is in your employ. I am worried my lord,' she paused, tilting her head down. She raised it to look into his eyes, 'I have heard nothing of him since he was conscripted by you nearly three years ago.'

'What is it you want to know?' he asked, walking around her, closely eyeing every part of her as she spoke.

'What do I want to know? Is that not obvious? Where is he, of course, and why does he not come home? What keeps my husband, a loving man, silent for so long?'

'Do you receive silver each turn of the moon?'

'Yes.'

'Then he is at his work.'

That's it?' she was now angry at this man who seemed to care not one jot for her worries.

'What more is there? Your husband, Suni, is my first mason. He must work to complete the temple commission by the Lady Hatshepsut. What she demands must be done,' he shrugged.

'I want to go to him, to see him, to be with him,' her tone began angrily, but became an almost beseeching plea.

'I am sorry for you, of course, but it will not be possible.'

'Why?' she demanded.

'He has taken an oath to keep the temple site secret. It is a vow he cannot break, and you cannot go there and must never know of its whereabouts. So just be patient, and when all is complete, when his work is done, you will be together again,'

'No!' she shouted.

He was about to dismiss her completely and tolerate her insolence no longer, when he saw from the corner of his eye. Lady Hatshepsut enter the room behind Mat'tan. He grabbed Mat'tan and thrust her to the ground, pressing her head face down to the floor.

'Your pharaoh is present. Keep your forehead to the floor in her presence' he commanded.

Seni also knelt and touched the floor with his forehead.

'I am honoured, my lady,' he said, without moving from his obeisant position.

Hatshepsut sat on the throne. She was completely naked apart from her jewellery.

'Rise, stonemason, and bring the pretty thing closer so I may look on your guest' she commanded.

There was an unmistakable tease in the voice of the pharaoh queen as she addressed Seni. Mat'tan recalled that there had been rumours even in the Necropolis about the lord mason and the Lady Hatshepsut being lovers.

The lord mason lifted Mat'tan gently and whispered, 'Do not look upon your queen. Keep your eyes downcast,' he warned.

'What is your name, child?' the queen asked.

'Mat'tan,' she answered, focusing on the floor.

'Mat'tan, my lady,' Seni corrected her.

'There is no need for formality today. Lift your head, Mat'tan,' the pharaoh queen spoke gently to her guest.

Mat'tan lifted her head as commanded, and saw the pharaoh to be without any clothing and young, only her own age. Out of sheer embarrassment, Mat'tan looked away. At this, Seni laughed out loud.

'It seems my guest is shy, my lady!' he smirked.

Mat'tan flushed, not with embarrassment, but with anger.

'I am not shy, but what am I to do when I look upon a living god who could be my sister?'

'Sister!' Seni spat the word out and raised his hand to strike Mat'tan.

'Hold, it is not her fault. She is not of the court and does not know any better,' she intervened.

'I am sorry. I meant no offence, my lady.'

'None taken, child. I think we need time alone away from this man. Leave us, stonemason. I will talk with Mat'tan and who knows, maybe I will grant her wish if it pleases me.'

Seni began to protest, but the lady Hatshepsut raised her hand, and he fell silent and left.

Mat'tan was amazed and baffled by what was unfolding. She found herself staring at her pharaoh, and realised she was an exceptionally beautiful woman. Surely men would do anything for her, she thought.

'Sister,' the lady Hatshepsut giggled. 'I like that. Maybe we are.' She then took Mat'tan's hand and led her into the Pharaoh's private quarters. That night Mat'tan was bathed by the Pharaoh's own attendants and dined with Hatshepsut in private. They talked and talked the night through as if she had always known the living god, as a friend, sister, or confidante. Mat'tan fell into a heavy sleep in the early hours of the morning, deep in slumber in the Pharaoh's chamber.

Mat'tan slept until midday, and when she awoke, she was dazed and her head ached from the large quantity of lotus wine consumed the night before. As she gained her senses she realised she had spent the entire night in the bed of the pharaoh, who was now gone. As she lifted herself wearily from the bed, she also realised she was naked. At this discovery, panic overcame her as she tried to recall what had passed during the night, but she could not. There was no memory. One minute she was wining, dining and laughing in the company of a god, then she was awake, a little unwell, but now wide awake.

Mat'tan quickly searched for her clothes, but they were nowhere to be found. Then she heard someone coming, so she swiftly pulled the bed-clothes up around her. Two handmaidens entered the chamber and again led her to a bath. Once more she was bathed and given new clothes, and then taken to a garden where the pharaoh and Seni were dining with several other people. All were dressed as soldiers, and even the pharaoh was wearing a rich, blue kilt and a golden breastplate.

'Come, Mat'tan. Sit with me!' she urged. It sounded more like a demand than request from the pharaoh. 'I have decided you will come with us today, and be re-united with your husband.'

Mat'tan was overjoyed at the news and impulsively kissed and hugged her pharaoh. The lord mason and the generals fell silent at the impertinence of Mat'tan.

'See, am I not a popular queen when my people love me so?' she bellowed.

The tension around the table eased and conversation broke out again.

'Oh, thank you, thank you!' Mat'tan repeated delightedly, squeezing her Pharaoh's hand.

Seni glowered at his lady It was a glance that was noted by all present.

Soon they were on their way, the journey beginning with pomp and ceremony as Mat'tan found herself aboard the Pharaoh's spacious chariot, drawn by four black steeds, followed by the Falcon chariot squadron and several legions of infantry.

What Mat'tan did not know was that another Season of the Hyena was about to fall on Egypt, a time of war. The pharaoh was on her way to the temple of her dead husband, Tuthmoses II. This was only a detour on her way to wage war, a war that would eventually not only rid Egypt of enemies from the North East, but would also confirm Hatshepsut as a great and living god, the first woman to reign as pharaoh without a king for centuries, and the usurper of the young Tuthmoses III.

Mat'tan was no longer overwhelmed by the extremity of all that had happened in just two short days. She was enjoying the ride even if it would not last. Also, soon she would be with Suni, and in his loving arms. The journey to the temple took three days and nights, and passed without incident, though news had been brought by messenger of a battle raging, as the Pharaoh's army repelled invading armies coming out of Canaan, who were allied with the Mitanni.

Mat'tan was at a loss to know exactly where they were. The desert was vast and for days she had seen nothing but sand under a scorching sun, setting up camp before the last glimmer of light every evening.

She was truly amazed when they arrived at the temple. It just seemed to appear out of nowhere. The temple had been built out of rock into the mountainside, and yet it appeared to have been built from stone independent of the mountain. It was an illusion and yet real, at the same time impossible to find, and discreetly guarded to protect it from treasure hunters and thieves, Seni had explained.

The lady Hatshepsut went alone to the chamber of her late husband, whilst Seni led Mat'tan to the ongoing work where she would find her husband.

Mat'tan came to the end of a long corridor and stepped into a large chamber full of beautifully carved statues of the gods, all in glistening black marble, with the walls depicting colourful images of the royal life, showing the pharaoh with impossible masculine proportions, as well as astrological constellations and victories in battle. The whole room was marvellously well lit by torches and polished metal. It was like daylight.

More than a dozen artists and master masons were occupied in their perfect and precise work. The atmosphere was almost magical.

'Carry on, my lovelies,' barked Seni on entering the chamber. 'Is it not a wonder to see?' he whispered to Mat'tan.

She was awe-struck and simply nodded as she continued to stare.

'Master Suni,' the lord stonemason bawled.

'You have a visitor. Come, do not keep a lady waiting.'

Suddenly, Suni appeared out of a group huddled around a partly carved statue, he clasped papyrus and a cubit stick in his hand.

'My lord, I am honoured by your patronage and presence,' he looked at Seni's attractive guest, but had no idea who the lady in fine clothes was. She was beautiful and reminded him of his wife, whom he dreamed of each night, but whom he had to learn to live without in his loneliness.

'You do not know my guest?' asked Seni, amusedly.

Before the question was even out, Suni realised that he was being confronted by an impossibility. It was just like dreams he many times. His wife stood before him. It really was her!

Mat'tan was now crying and her stomach was rolling and spinning. Her whole body was tingling with nervous excitement. They embraced and kissed, then suddenly, Suni pushed her back.

'Why?'

He was looking at his master.

'The pharaoh wished it so, and so it is.'

'But I don't understand!' expostulated Suni.

'There is nothing to understand. Are you not happy?'

'Yes, but it just is not possible!' he sighed, his voice quaking with emotion.

'For pharaoh, all is possible,' Seni grinned, before leaving them to inspect the work so far.

Suni listened as Mat'tan told him of how she came to be with him and how the Lady Hatshepsut had given her blessing and made her welcome in the palace, but for some reason, she was not really sure why, she instinctively avoided any mention of sleeping in the Pharaoh's bed.

They went to Suni's quarters which were cool and comfortable, if a little austere.

'I am so happy to see you, my wife, but I fear it is not a good thing,'

'What are you saying? Why are you distressed to be with me?' she asked anxiously.

Suni could not hide the worry he felt. His face made it plain.

'I am happy to be with you, so very happy, but it makes no sense for the Lord Seni to bring you here.'

'Why? What is wrong? Why are you so worried?'

'I do not know, except you are the first and only person to come here apart from builders, artists, soldiers and aristocrats, and those who have a direct connection with the construction of the temple. It makes me fearful.'

'But come, my husband, we are together.'

Mat'tan embraced her husband and they kissed passionately."

Darragh blinked his eyes open and sighed.

"I think that's enough," he remarked.

"Fine," I replied, but I knew there was more, so I asked, "Do you need a break before you continue?"

He flushed, then grinned.

"They were about to make love so I thought it was time to be discreet!" he explained.

"Will you continue with the regression?" I urged.

"Oh, yes. I would just like a cup of tea first," he said.

Darragh took the break, and once refreshed, relaxed again and retired to the trance state.

"I am in pain," he complained.

"Darragh, Darragh, can you hear me?" I asked him with increasing concern.

"Pain," he moaned.

"Darragh, relax, relax," I spoke the words slowly and softly.

"It's okay," he murmured.

With his eyes closed, Darragh began to talk again.

"Sorry, for a moment I was feeling a burning pain in my stomach, but it has passed now. I am with Mat'tan again. She is in a dark corridor carrying a torch and following Suni. They are leaving the light less corridor and emerging into a mountain plateau in the desert above the temple site. A lot has happened over those days during which the pharaoh quashed the invading armies in the North East. Several squadrons of Canaanite charioteers have seized and overrun the temple.

Mat'tan and Suni have no choice now but to run and hide in the desert mountains. So far they have been lucky to survive the attack. As far as they know, everyone was left for dead, slain without mercy by the invaders. Night was falling and the temperature was dropping, due to the high altitude. They had no protection or shelter from the elements, so reluctantly they made their way back to the passageway from whence they came. Their hope was that no one had found the corridor, and they could shelter safely. This was not to be. In the shadow of the half moon sky they could see figures emerging from the corridor onto the plateau. They lay flattened against the sandy ground of the mountain top. But there was no cover, no hiding place. All they were certain of was that, as long as they lay still, they could not be seen - providing no one came their way.

Alas, it seemed the gods were conspiring against them. The figures now held torches and were heading towards them.

'We must run from here. It is our only hope,' Suni whispered, already breathless. He took Mat'tan's hand and they ran away from the approaching torches. Though they did not know it, they were heading for a ravine hidden from view by a trick of the night light. In just a few hundred breathless steps, they ran hand in hand into mid-air and began to fall, screaming all the way down. Mat'tan lost all sensation as she fell.

There was no measure of time. It could have been hours or even a day. Gradually feelings came back until all her senses were responding. She opened her eyes to see a clear, pale blue sky Before she moved to stand, she felt Suni's hand in hers. She released the grip and stood up startled to be alive after falling from the immense mountain.

She looked down at her husband. He looked as though he was asleep. He was breathing gently and, amazingly, looked unhurt, though this could not of course, be possible.

She knelt down. 'Suni, Suni wake up,' she spoke the words softly and then shook him.

'Husband, wake!' she tried again.

He moaned and then let out a distressed scream that suggested he thought he was still falling. Suddenly, and without warning, he jumped to his feet.

'What!' he shouted, stunned by the shock of being alive.

'Be calm, husband,' she soothingly urged.

'What is this? Where are we? We fell last night, in the dark!' he stammered.

'I know, but here we are. I think this must be the Afterlife. We must have travelled into the West.'

'But it is daylight, and where is Anubis to weigh our souls?' he persisted in confusion.

'I don't know,' she quavered.

Mat'tan and Suni were standing in an oasis, and for the first time they realised they were not alone. Several other people were relaxing in the shade, while others took water and ate fruit. Astonishingly, animals that ordinarily should not share oasis water together were free to drink and graze. There were lions, hyenas, gazelle and buffalo, all drinking side by side.

Instinctively, Mat'tan and her husband went to the water, to sup and to bathe. Before they could stoop to the water, a hooded man stuck out his arm to stop them.

'This is not for you. You must go there,' he said, and he pointed out of the oasis and into the desert.

'But we are thirsty,' protested Suni.

'Do not delay. Go into the West. Speak to no one here. This place is not for you.'

The hooded stranger spoke slowly, with an accent neither of them had heard before. Nevertheless they seemed to trust him, so without quenching their thirst, they followed the direction they were bidden.

Mat'tan and Suni walked through soft sand that made each step a heavy trudge. As they stumbled over undulating dunes, night fell suddenly without the transition of twilight. A wind began lifting the sand into their faces, then the wind began to howl as a storm whipped up the sand around them, stinging their flesh.

They huddled together and lay in the nape of a dune to escape the work of this blinding, painful sandstorm.

'What is happening to us? Are we not to go into the West, the Afterlife, and to live in the Garden of the Gods?' Mat'tan sobbed as she bemoaned their plight.

'No, my love, it is just the journey to the West. This may be the scales of Anubis as he weighs our souls' Suni assured her.

'What if we are not worthy to live again with the loved ones who have travelled there already? We fell to our deaths in some valley and our bodies may never be found and therefore made ready for the Underworld' said Mat'tan sorrowfully.

'Do not fret so. We are good people. We live, lived, our lives honourably. We will soon be in the Garden of the Gods.'

'I am afraid.'

Mat'tan held her husband more tightly in an attempt to ease her anxiety.

The storm stopped suddenly and the night sky was clear with brilliant stars and a full moon low on the horizon, looking twice its usual size and glowing amber. They stood and brushed themselves free of sand.

'Look!' Mat'tan pointed to a pyramid on the horizon. 'What is it?' she asked, squinting to focus into the distance.

'It is one of the great temples of the old pharaohs. They used to build them, but we have lost the knowledge of their construction. They are now a great mystery to us.'

The pyramid was a brilliant white, but glowed pale blue in the starry night light.

'Are we to go there?' Mat'tan asked.

'It seems so, my wife.'

They set off in the direction of the pyramid. This time the sand was firm and their step sure. In what seemed like no time at all they were at the base of the pyramid which almost filled their vision, and loomed up into the sky. It seemed to actually touch the sky.

They walked around the pyramid's base, completing a circuit of its four sides, each equal and straight, tapering to a point within the sky. Its sides were smooth and now they were up close they could see that it was brilliant white.

As they craned their necks upwards, the night sky filled with a brilliant light show as a meteor shower lit up the sky with shooting stars; an aurora of purple, turquoise, orange and pink waves across the sky appeared in breathtaking beauty.

'What a night!' Mat'tan gasped with awed wonder.

'This must be it, the Gardens,' Suni thought aloud.

'No, but it is the gateway,' came a voice they recognised instantly. It was that of the hooded man from the oasis. Both Mat'tan and Suni looked about them, but saw no one. Then a hiss like that of a snake was heard all around them. They held each other tightly.

Suddenly, a crack of light appeared in the pyramid, growing from base to tip and becoming more brilliant, finally widening to the width of ten men.

At first it was so bright that they had to guard their eyes as they were bathed in the ethereal light. Then, just as suddenly the light dimmed, allowing them to see once more. There before them was the hooded man again. In one hand he held a staff from which an eerie light emanated. In the other he held a pair of scales.

'Anubis.'

The name was whispered on Mat'tan and Suni's lips simultaneously.

Anubis held out his scales and at that moment both Mat'tan and Suni's bodies began to glow. Each chakra lit up and spun giving out beams of light joining together into a sphere of light in front of them, ready to be weighed and judged by Anubis.

Suni's soul moved gently through the air and rested upon the left plate of the Libran scale. At that same moment, a large blue peacock feather appeared on the right plate of the scales. The hood fell from Anubis's head revealing his head to be that of a jackal, jet black with burning red eyes, which were watching for any movement on the scale.

There was none, and the soul of Suni floated in a spiral and disappeared into the pyramid.

Now the jackal-headed Anubis gazed upon Mat'tan. Her soul moved towards the left plate of the Libran scale. The light of her soul rested. Anubis watched the soul. The scales began to quiver. The peacock feather fluttered. Mat'tan gasped. Worry surged through every fibre of her body and her mind raced. Guilt gripped her stomach and a memory of the night she had spent in the bed of the pharaoh queen, and the three nights in the desert which she had dismissed from her mind under the influence of lotus wine, now came thumping into her consciousness.

Anubis, with eyes blazing, grinned, baring terrifying sharp fangs. As the left plate began to fall, the feather began to rise from the right plate of the scale. Mat'tan knew in that instant she was destined never to travel into the West and the Garden of the Afterlife. She was about to swoon in her despair when suddenly, Isis appeared at the side of Anubis and lifted the scales into balance. The soul of Mat'tan began to glow brilliantly and then like the soul of her husband her soul also ascended, spiralling lightly into the pyramid."

Darragh fell silent. After a few moments he opened his eyes. Slightly bemused, he looked at his hands and exclaimed,

"My goodness! I have never been so frightened!" he shuddered.

"I'm not surprised," I answered reassuringly.

"I cannot accept all I have seen, felt and said, but I assure you it is real. I know everything about her and the others. It is not a dream or fantasy, but a tangible thing. What's more, I had all her emotions inside me, and believe me when I say that when Anubis was weighing Mat'tan's soul I thought I, she, was to be damned. You have no idea how amazed and relieved I was when Isis arrived and saved me, I mean Mat'tan, but you know that was me!" he smiled.

"Do you remember what happened after that?" I asked, thoroughly captivated and intrigued.

"I don't, yet I have an impression of joy; sorry I can't make it clearer than that," he shrugged, content with the knowledge he had just gained.

Darragh has since recalled several past lives, none of which has been quite so dramatic as the life he remembers as Mat'tan. He developed his skills and now uses regression therapy in his work as a counsellor and healer.

Marine's Story

White Woman Walking

I was teaching my last workshop for the year at Edinburgh Castle Conference Centre. The snow had been falling since early morning.

Only two delegates on the workshop were from Britain, the rest from the four corners of the globe: America, Brazil, Canada, Indonesia, New Zealand and one from France; Marine, a television producer who specialised in language education programmes. She was most enthusiastic about everything to the point of annoyance to everyone else, despite her willingness to volunteer as a subject for past life regression.

Marine responded to the Heart, Light, Harmony State method wonderfully and easily entered a deep altered state. As I began to quiz her on all she saw, something interesting happened - she replied in French. No matter how much I urged her to speak in English she persisted in using French. This was not a problem for everyone else as they all spoke several languages including French. Only one of the Americans and myself were at a loss as to what she was saying.

I brought the session to an end. Marine opened her eyes, yawned and stretched as though she was waking from a long night's sleep. For a moment she looked puzzled, unaware of her surroundings. Then the reality of where she was came to her.

"Magnifique!" she exclaimed.

"How are you?" I asked.

"Bonne."

"Why are you speaking in French and not English?" I inquired.

"Pardon. Sorry. I was not thinking about how I was speaking, I suppose. I think in French, so I guess it must be natural to respond in French," she explained.

"Do you think it would be possible to reply to me in English during the past life regression?" I asked.

"I don't see why not. I will try," she smiled.

"What can you remember from the session you just experienced?"

I was keen to know all the details of what she had just witnessed.

"Of course, yes, I was a child. I was out in the country, by the side of a river. It was summer and very hot. There were tall trees, I could smell fish cooking on the opposite bank of the river. Mountains, they were so high that snow covered the peaks. Not the Alps. I could see for many, many kilometres ..." her voice faded as she recalled the beautiful scene.

"Where do you think you were?" I asked encouragingly.

"I do not think ..." she became vague for a moment. Her eyes widened, "\ know. Now I understand why I spoke in French and not in English. When I was little I used to have dreams about the place I saw. I used to say I lived there before I was born. My parents and teachers told me to stop saying such things as it was nonsense, the imaginings of a silly girl. So I forgot them. These memories of a past life in my childhood have resurfaced," she asserted.

"I see. What has happened here is not a past life recall but suppressed memories from your childhood. That explains why your response was in French, because those memories were from a time when the only language you knew was your native tongue," I reassured her.

"What are you saying? Are you telling me that these are false memories or just childhood imaginings?" Her tone became quite indignant.

"No, not at all. Tell me all you remember so far, then we can assess everything."

She pulled her lips down at the corners and shrugged her shoulders in a comic caricature of French mime.

"If you say so," she replied haughtily, rolling her eyes and exaggerating her accent.

I looked out of one of the two small windows in the room. My heart sank. Night was falling and the snow flurries were becoming heavier. It was not going to be easy to drive back to Newton in time for the new year celebrations with my family.

I estimated that if we could complete everything in less than two hours and the roads turned out to be not so bad, I might just make it back in time. I put the issue to the rest of room,

"Obviously, we will run a little late today if we explore Marine's past life. Let us have a show of hands about this and see if everyone wants to continue."

Instantly, everyone's hands shot up. It was unanimous, we all wanted to hear Marine's story.

Before she entered the altered state Marine gave us an account of what used to happen when she was a little girl living in Ottange in eastern France, close to the border with Luxembourg. Both her parents had worked there, her father being a banker and her mother a restaurateur.

"One day, I remember now, yes, I remember it very well. It is odd to think I put this out of my mind. I would have been six, maybe seven years of age. The teacher was talking about Red Indians and how they were savages until the French went to the Americans and gave them Christianity and a civilisation of life. I remember feeling defensive and standing up and shouting at the teacher, saying 'you are lying; we are not savages. We are good people; it is you and your type that brought disease and death, not good things'. I was crying all the time I was protesting. You see what I dreamt about and remembered as a child was real to me and now I see that, but then people thought me a silly girl with a head full of nonsense. I now realise that I suppressed those memories so as to fit in. I wish I had not."

Marine paused, taking a slow, deep breath.

"D'accord, monsieur. I am ready to begin."

I led her through the regression method but made sure I added a suggestion that she spoke in English only.

Once Marine was in the altered state I began by asking her to tell me exactly what she saw. There was no need to question her further, straight away Marine began speaking with ease and in detail about everything she was seeing.

"I feel the wind. It is strong tonight. They will come, bringing death and sorrow. My uncle, a great warrior, a man of honour who is loved for his courage, strength and wisdom, speaks to the Council of Elders. He says these so-called Sioux are not like us. We are Oglala Sioux, we respect the spirits of our fathers and all that lives. These are not of our lineage though they have the same tongue. They are not brothers or cousins, but men without honour, so we cannot trust them. He speaks the truth. I have seen it in a vision when the night is at its blackest with no moon and clouds of rain hiding the stars. They come on horseback with death and blood in their hearts."

Marine paused, so I took the opportunity to clarify what she was seeing, "Who is your uncle, and what may I call you?"

"Spirit Walking Bear is my uncle. He has the medicine strong within him. He teaches me the language of visions and my name is White Day, but soon I will take my personal name. White Woman Walking.

I am afraid for my people and am to speak with the elders this day and talk of the danger my uncle knows and I have seen in my vision. Alas, they do not accept what we warn, so we must stay here. There is to be one more moon before we travel south ahead of the winter. I know this is a mistake but the Council of Elders say we are strong enough to repel the raiders who they see as a band of mischievous outcasts without bravery. I do not want to die so have taken permission to travel alone to the yellow rock caves, a sacred place where hot springs and steam sweats the body. This is a sacred place for men and women of the medicine visions.

I set off on foot alone. I am well aware that it is going to take three days before I reach the yellow rock; this will be enough time to purge my body ready for the vision quest. I will eat no food on the journey and drink water only where my grandfather's spirit provides it.

I am excited. The yellow rock is high and the cave of sweat is a steep climb. I decide to bathe first, in the hot pools that rise at the base of this sacred rock.

After more than three days of fasting my body is cleansed inside and, with the hot water, now clean outside. I am ready for my quest. My body is weak as I climb up the yellow rock to the cave. Once inside, the precious silence is only disturbed by the gurgling of the hot water rising and steam hissing from fissures in the rock walls. There is no light at all in the cave, but I know its form like my own hand.

Despite the darkness I find the plinth ledge set high in the cave, a hot spot within the hot cave. I sit myself down, with my legs crossed resting my wrists on my knees, then I begin to breathe the hot air. At first it burns my nostrils and throat, but this soon passes and I lose all sense of time. The heat makes me weak and draws sweat from my body. I choose the mountain cat to guide me in my vision. In the dense blackness of the cave the mountain cat sits opposite me. My thoughts are aimed into the cat. My body sways as my mind swims in a sea of brilliant colours from the Wakan, the spirit of my forefathers in my head. I see lightning strike, then I am the mountain cat.

I swiftly stride out of the cave and up to the top of the rock. This is the unfolding of my vision quest. My body is still silent, unmoving, while my mind and spirit are invigorated, free. As I wait in the image of my totem animal I begin to feel like a cat and think like a cat. I know I must be as the mountain cat and be ready to walk with the spirits who also take a totem animal shape.

A wolf appears to me, the totem animal of my grandmother. The wolf begins to run and I follow. The strength and agility of the mountain cat surges through me. Lightning flashes and the thunder roars as I follow the powerful wolf. The wolf slows, so do I. The wolf stops, so do I.

Following the wolf's gaze, my vision falls upon a bison of dazzling white. The brilliance of the bison glows increasingly, before transforming into a beautiful woman. I become aware that this female before me was the first woman to give birth to my nation and some say the nation of all the two-legged people. She is the grandmother of all two-legged people. All who are born can walk with her and be touched by her sacred spirit.

Then, the wolf is no more. I am alone with my ancestor. She holds out her hands and in them she holds a bundle wrapped in golden yellow hide tied neatly with red leather bindings.

The vision gently fades as I reach out for the gift she offers me. Suddenly, I am hot again, back in the sweat cave of the yellow rock mountain. The intense smell of the earth is on my body as I leave the cave and step into the rising sun of the dawn. At the mouth of the cave floor there is a bundle, the very same bundle I had seen in my vision quest. I pick up the hide bundle. It is the softest hide I have ever felt and surprisingly heavy. Cross-legged I sit in the spot where I found the bundle, looking out from this mountain of yellow rock.

As I take in the scene before me, I am aware that the beauty of the landscape has never been so remarkable. From the east the sun begins to light the mountains and evergreen forest which bathes good and pure air in a magical mist. To the south grass plains are awakening with bison, deer and numerous unseen beasts. The sound of the fast flowing river fills the air as it runs south from the mountains, then across the high plain. To the east the forest shines brilliant green in the reflection of the sun, but it is too cool yet for the birds to take flight. Nonetheless, their chattering and singing adds another layer to the breathtaking beauty of this sacred land.

I lift the hide parcel above my head and thank my ancestors for the gift. The unwrapping of the parcel is done with reverence by me, and as the hide opens I find a pipe made from horn and carved with symbols of the ancestors whose meanings are sacred, but alas, lost to us now. At the base of the bowl and the mouthpiece, feathers of the speckled eagle hang loose in adornment of this peace-giving pipe. Also in the parcel is tobacco which when smoked gives truth to the user of the pipe. Next to this lies an obsidian bladed stone fashioned in the shape of a bear's claw. A medicine pouch containing sweet grasses and wild sage is decorated with many coloured beads depicting a sun with four lightning arrows representing the four directions of the wind above a blue lake held in a green valley. Thus fire, air, water and earth are represented on the pouch. Its straps are wrapped around a smooth pebble of banded agate with seven red circles painted on one side.

I place the medicine pouch around my neck, then open a satchel and remove dried bison meat and a skin bag containing spring water. This is the first meal since I have set forth on my vision quest. I gather up everything and set off to rejoin my people with the hope all will be well."

Marine's recollection had everyone in the room captivated. We were all eager to hear where the events would take her. She spoke on,

"It took me three long days to get back. What met me when I arrived was to break my heart so completely I would never again be the same.

No teepee was left standing, nor the lodge of the elders. Everywhere was barren, just smouldering ashes; worse ahead, smoking bodies of the people I loved lay amid an acrid and putrid chaotic massacre of more than two hundred Sioux of my blood.

Already the fowl of the air and the beasts of the land were about, returning my now dead relatives to the four corners. I raised my hands to the sky and prayed for all their souls to travel into the Happy Land.

Heavy footed, I slowly walked away to the east and south following the trail left by the murderers of my nation. I did not look back. I did not need to, the dark clouds rolled in, thunder and lightning bellowed from the sky and then the heavens opened and poured forth a torrential deluge. Everything that had happened here was to be washed away, leaving no trace of my nation. Only I now carried the knowledge of our ancestors. I needed to find new and good people, an honourable nation tribe who lived the way of the Sioux and Wakan.

I walked for six days, all but one of them full of rainfall. The rain had obliterated any tracks, so I followed the river on the high side. The plentiful evergreens on the high bank allowed me cover. It was on that sixth day that I found others. They had already crossed the river and had set their camp on a clearing close to the river. Their teepees were lazily erected without attention to direction, the openings were not uniform and only one was set sunwise. All seemed unclean, like them. Though they were dressed in the way and style of the Sioux, their habits were not Sioux. These people were without spirit. I had to do something."

Marine opened her eyes and let out a piercing shout. She looked totally drained as she began to cry uncontrollably. I held her to calm her. Eventually she relaxed into gentle sobs and sighs.

"It hurts so much. I miss them. I feel all the sorrow, " she murmured.

"It's okay now. You are back here in the present, in Edinburgh." I reassured her.

Marine looked around at all who were present. She was clutching herself as if she was cold, then closed her eyes.

"Merci," she whispered, then sat herself upright. "I will stop now. I am tired, but tomorrow I wish to continue."

"That will not be possible. I travel back to England this evening, but at the end of January I will be here again," I explained.

"Then I will wait."

Everyone left the lecture room together chatting enthusiastically about what had transpired during Marine's regression. I collected my things together and wasted no time myself in leaving. The snow was now falling in swirling flurries to the sound of a lone piper on the castle wall. It took me a little while to negotiate the curving downhill road that led from the rear of the castle before I emerged into the city of Edinburgh traffic which was surprisingly busy. Time was tight and I fretted about returning to Newton before midnight. Thankfully, I made it home with half an hour to spare and was soon joining in the New Year celebrations, even if I was a little tired.

That night sleep came to me quickly. I had gone to bed at 2am. However, at 4.30am I woke with a start. I was covered in sweat and felt uncomfortably unaware of my surroundings. The dream I was having had not broken and as I drifted back to sleep the dream continued.

I found that I was surrounded by thick smoke and I could distinctly hear bees buzzing. The smoke gradually cleared. I was alone in a sweat lodge and completely naked apart from a buckskin loincloth. I found myself drawn to the smouldering embers of a fire set in the centre of the lodge, which my gazed fixed upon. Then, from outside I heard the steady beat of drums and the wailing of Sioux chanting. The rhythm of the drums and chanting filled my head.

I began to dance the Eagle Dance, with my arms spread and mimicking the eagle's wings. I shuffled, hopped, skipped and swooped in swirling circles. My head tilted this way and that, just as elegantly as the eagle's would.

Suddenly, I found I was outside the sweat lodge and fully clothed in ornate buckskin trousers, wearing a shirt covered in beadwork with also a headdress of turkey feathers. The dance became more fevered, as the chanting and drumming merged into a spiritual crescendo. Nearby, I could see the sun rising on a purple dawn, then the sun was high and colour flooded the landscape. I felt the rush of wind.

Next, I leapt into the sky from some heady eyrie. I was changed. I had become an eagle. The thermals lifted me and fear spun my stomach as I looked out below me at the vastness of the plains, beautiful flat-topped mountains of red and yellow stood out of the grass-covered plain and a river ran a deep gouge through the land. I seemed to be following the river to its source where a forest of tall pines gathered along the sides of the snow-topped Wind River Mountains. With my eagle eyes my focus fell on a herd of bison as they fed on the grasses, it sharpened as I picked out a white bison. I began to swoop with a vertical drop of lightning speed, blurring the view of the creature.

I jumped! I found I was suddenly awake in my bed, my heart pulsating excessively as I panted for breath. The phone had started ringing, and whilst my wife answered the call, I went to the bathroom and threw cold water over my face to try and calm myself. I brushed a tremoring hand through my hair and watched in amazement as a small feather floated down into the wash basin.

"It's for you," my wife called.

"Take a message!" I snapped, walking into the bedroom in confusion.

"She insists that you speak to her now," my wife urged as she handed me the phone.

"Okay," I sighed rubbing my eyes tiredly. "Hello, Raymond speaking."

I was surprised to hear that it was Marine. She politely asked me if I could see her that day. I explained this would not be possible, after all, it was New Year's Day. However, we agreed to meet up again on the third of January. Just before she hung up she unexpectedly said something that struck me as curious. Marine quickly told me how she had dreamt about her past life regression that night. Stranger still, in her dream she had specifically seen me performing the Eagle Dance.

As I returned to the bedroom, my wife exclaimed as she pointed to my legs,

"What on earth have you done to yourself?"

I looked down to see that both of my legs were marked with several deep scratches. The fresh wounds were still seeping blood.

At that moment I knew my so-called dream had in fact been an out-of-body experience, the scratches being a common sign for shamans after out-of-body experiences, not to mention the unbelievable presence of the feather as well as also appearing in someone else's dream. This experience was a first for me in adult life. Not since childhood had I had clear out-of-body experiences. As I confided the night's incidents to my wife she was not at all alarmed, as she herself has out-of-body experiences frequently and with ease.

It was midday on the third of January when Marine arrived at my studio in Liverpool. The snow had entirely melted away after the heavy fall over the New Year holiday. After several apologies and pardons, she started to tell me a dream she had recalled recently. She explained to me that she had fallen asleep early on New Year's Eve/Day,

" ...So it must have been well after two o'clock in the morning by the time I eventually went to sleep. It seemed that no sooner were my eyes closed, than I was dreaming. I suppose quite naturally in the circumstances, I was dreaming of my past life. I was the young native American woman again, but it was a time before the massacre of my people. There was a great gathering of people and a feast. My uncle was dancing the Eagle Dance, but his face was your face. I do not mean exactly the same face, I mean it was you from a previous life - I recognised the energy. What are your thoughts on this?" she asked excitedly.

I paused, somewhat unsettled by the inconceivability of what she was saying.

"It is of course possible, but I have no recollection of a native American past life with the Sioux," I lied. I chose not to mention my dream which strangely seemed to synchronise with Marine's.

Marine was insistent,

"It was you. I have no doubt. Also, I remembered more of the regression from the workshop. I think I know why I escaped the massacre of my people in that past life. I communicated with Wakan Tanka, a sacred woman who used spirit wisdom and walked with the ancestors. I also understand now why I became upset and angry when as a child I would hear terrible things said about so-called Red Indians, so even as a child I felt the need to be identified with the native Americans," she justified sincerely.

"Yes. I understand the affinity of which you speak. It is often the case that people remember feelings and emotions rather than actual people and places," I assured her, still a little distracted.

"No. It is more than that. When teachers taught history they would say Europeans brought civilisation and Christianity to heathens and barbarians. This was not true, all they brought was conquest, bad laws and terrible diseases that killed many of the native people. In some cases whole societies were wiped off the face of the land. I knew all this even as a small child."

"I see. It seems this channel to that past life has always been open to you then," I surmised.

Marine expressed much keenness to enter a regression again and to explore her past life in as much detail as she possibly could.

"Very well," I agreed, also interested to know more. "We can do that now, if you like. Are you ready?"

Marine got herself comfortable and soon closed her eyes. She quickly entered the altered state of awareness.

"I am cold," she said hugging herself.

"What do you see?" I asked.

"Nothing. It is just blackness and cold. No, wait. I can see colours, lights of colour."

She fell silent, then leant in closer to hush me,

"Be quiet, or they will find me."

"Who will?" I whispered.

"It is all right. They have passed." She gasped the words as she spoke. "I had to hide in the water. They must not know that I watch them. But the water is cold," Marine shivered.

"Who is it you are following?" I asked.

"The deadly horsemen, the killing thieves who massacred my people. It has been one moon since their attack. I have witnessed more brutality by them during that time. I cannot stop them alone. It is time to ask my ancestors to intervene, to use their power to destroy these heartless men."

Marine suddenly opened her eyes.

"Lord, I know what it is she does," she exclaimed.

"Sorry, you've lost me," I said, now mystified.

"Pardon," she paused. "Just then, when I was seeing my past life, I could feel everything, see everything, then suddenly all of her life was in my head in a split second. Everything. She fights fire with fire. She evokes the fire spirit to cause havoc to them."

"I think you need to explain further," I urged her.

"But of course."

Marine sat back and closed her eyes and began to breathe deeply. Before she talked she clenched her teeth as if grimacing in anticipation of something distressful. Marine let out a nervous vibrato scream, then sighed.

"I am the spirit that is both White Woman Walking and Marine. I am Alet. I have lived many lives but eventually I am in Marine."

Marine said nothing more for the next eight long minutes. Then she broke the powerful silence,

"I can tell you everything now. White Woman Walking had become very weak and after hiding from the raiders in the water, she sought help. She made her way to a Lakota village at the foot of the Wind River Mountains. It was there that she performed the Sun Dance and conjured up a power to defeat the outcast raiders who had no spirit, only greed and self-serving intent. [The Sun Dance is a rare practice, even rarer when performed by women. It is used in times of danger by individuals to harness the strength of the ancestors, and give the dancer the ability to defeat their enemy or gain respect as a shaman.]

White Woman Walking prepared for the Sun Dance. On the first day she walked in the forest until she found the right tree. It had to be tall and straight but not too old. She found the right one while the sun was still low. She placed her arms around it and at a stretch her fingertips just touched. She held that position for some time and thanked the spirits for such a gift. Alone she felled the tree, removed all its branches and stripped the bark. She then cut it into three lengths, and painted each one red on the second day.

As the third day began she erected the frame, a tripod. At the apex which stood at twice her height, she placed twigs to represent the nest of the fire-bird. Before nightfall she had decorated the frame with images of fire-birds, suns and symbols from her dream time. That night she ate meat from the fore-shoulder of bison. After her meal she smoked sacred tobacco, then sat crossed-legged in front of a slow burning fire. She chanted the whole night through in communication with the Wakan Tanka, the spirit force of native Americans. This would prepare her mind, body and spirit for the arduous and painfully torturing Sun Dance.

Once day came, she remained in her position but had to stop chanting. She was waiting for the sun to rise above the tree line. Once this had happened she bathed in the river then dressed in new buckskin pants and shirt. She tied her hair back and dressed it with one feather from a speckled eagle. She then put a whistle fashioned from the wing bone of an eagle in her mouth. She threw two hide ropes over the tripod frame and checked them to ensure they were secure and would hold her weight. As the four ends of leather rope hung down, she picked up two, at the ends of which were fixed eagle claws. The whistle shrieked as she pierced her upper chest on the left side. The whistling continued, driving birds into the air as the claw broke skin. She repeated the act on the right side of her upper chest. It took a little longer to complete and was more painful. She waited for the blood to staunch, then tied the other two ends to a heavy log which rested atop a boulder.

Everything was in position for the Sun Dance. She began by ensuring that her position would have her facing the sun for the maximum time possible. She stared directly into the sun for as long as she could, her eyes watered as green and purple filled her vision, so she could see nothing, she was for a time blinded by the sunlight. In that state of blindness she pushed the log that was more than her body weight from the boulder. Instantly the leather ropes became taut and pulled her off her feet. The whistle between her teeth screamed as she breathed rapidly out and then in as the pain from the claws in her chest pulled against her weight. The pain put her into shock and for a few moments she lost consciousness. The pain came in waves of intolerable heat, followed by cold shivers as though she had plunged into icy water. She managed to lift her head in the direction of the sun but kept her eyes closed. Her head was full of visions of colour - red, green, blue, purple burst in bubbles and then white lightning streaked across her vision.

She lost consciousness again, this time the whistle fell from her lips, and she began to float free from her physical body. Her spirit had been set free through the endurance of the Sun Dance.

White Woman Walking was now travelling through the air without the limitations of her body. She could go anywhere her thoughts wanted to take her. In what was no more than a few seconds she had travelled a great distance to a mountain forest of great pines and in a forest clearing amongst these trees she saw her enemy, the heartless warriors who knew only theft and murder. In her out-of-body state she hovered above them praying to her ancestors to give her the strength to defeat them.

She began to chant and as she did so several of the men looked to the sky. At first it seemed they were looking at her, then she heard what had aroused them to look her way. Thunder roared and clouds moved in. Lightning arched in sky-filling veins across the sky. No rain fell as the thunder roared ever louder and the lightning forked ferociously to the ground striking one man in the centre of his head as he ran for cover. He burst into flames as he fell, causing the dry brush around him to ignite. A tirade of lightning bolts struck the ground and tree fires went up all around the camp. The men were running in every direction trying to escape this fiery carnage. Birds flew away from the fire and antelope, deer, bear and numerous other creatures escaped the ring of fire that had trapped the killing men.

White Woman Walking let out a scream as intolerable pain burned her chest. The weight of her body against the pull of the talon had eventually ripped the flesh from the right upper breast. The talon in her left chest held, but strained and pulled all the more. She was fully conscious but weak as blood flowed freely from the open wound on her chest. She reached for the obsidian blade in her belt with her right hand. After many attempts she gripped the blade but her hold was feeble as her fingers were numb. Mustering all the strength she could she lifted her arm and drew the blade across the leather rope. The sharpness of the blade against the taut rope cut it easily at the first stroke. White Woman Walking lay exhausted and weak in a heap below the tripod, her Sun Dance complete. She drifted into sleep with the chest wound still bleeding.

Meanwhile, a forest fire spread several miles in every direction, trapping and killing the band of Sioux outcasts who had terrorised the plains for two summers. Then, as threatened, the clouds burst in the heaviest downpour than had been seen in living memory. The flames were quenched leaving the forest safe.

An old man out hunting came upon White Woman Walking as she lay motionless in a pool of blood. Somehow she was not dead, though she should have been.

The man, despite his great age, was strong and able. He fashioned a litter after binding her wounds. He then felt at his own chest remembering his own Sun Dance many, many suns ago, but he had been lucky, he had not been alone, he had had his tribe, his blood, to attend him.

Once he secured her and her belongings on the litter, he strapped it to his horse and made for home. The day had turned to night before he brought her to his wigwam fashioned from skins and pelts. Inside it was comfortable, with plenty of room for a man living alone.

Several days passed during which he attended her. He used medicine of the forest and of the ancestors. He prayed to Wakan Tanka and beat a drum as he chanted. Every few hours he dripped the juice of berries mixed with spring-water into her mouth. Some was lost but most was drunk in an involuntary swallow by this brave woman, as he came to think of her. After three days she began to burn and sweat with fever.

White Woman Walking felt life leaving her. She was travelling in the sky, a sky of stars, but in the distance she could see a land. This was the Happy Hunting Ground of the ancestors, but as she reached out suddenly all became darkness. She felt pain as her body moved. Someone was moving her. She could hear mumbling and grunting, then just for the briefest moment the blackness went and colour came in. Within that colour there was a face, an old face of a man with lines so deep in it they could have been drawn there, then the blackness returned.

White Woman Walking felt heat, incredible heat and then cold as she was burning with a fever. In that fever nightmares began to haunt her fitful sleep. Death was close. She saw herself standing on a high mountain with clouds below her. She was afraid and held a light grip on a rock only for it to crumble away in her hands. Then her mind was distracted by a sound. It was the sound of wind, but unlike any she had heard before. In an instant she was blown from the mountain top. She was falling, endlessly falling into the unknown, into the clouds.

Then a searing pain hit her in the chest. An enormous eagle had dug its talons into her and began to fly away with her. The clouds suddenly burst open and she was hanging below the eagle soaring over the mountain forest, she could see smoke in the distance and then flames. There was the sound of thunder and lightning striking the tall trees of the forest, as fire spread everywhere. The eagle swooped into the forest flames then released its grip. Again White Woman Walking felt herself falling but this time she could see what was below her, a fire raging in the forest. She fell into the flames, her skin was burning, the heat penetrating her bones. She could see the scorched earth coming ever closer and the charred bodies of men, then - blackness.

White Woman Walking felt something cool on her lips and a bittersweet taste in her mouth. She opened her eyes but saw nothing. A voice whispered 'Easy, lie easy.' It was deep yet kind, like that of a grandfather. She felt her head being lifted and a spoon at her lips.

'Drink. It is good for you, brave one,' the same voice urged with concern and love.

Then she felt sleep wash over her again, and a vision came instantly to her. She saw a bright light which changed into a white bison, then back into a flame of white. In her head she heard a gentle woman's voice."

Marine suddenly forced herself upright, gasping for breath as though there was no air. She then sighed deeply and began to cry. I held her until the sorrow subsided and calm had returned to her. Her panicked breathing settled.

"Merci. Pardon. I am well, really, tres bonne, mon ami."

"You're okay? Are you sure?" I checked.

"Yes, I am. I was not crying with pain or upset. I am full of joy. I must tell you."

"Please do because I have some questions that I need to be answered, but you speak first, tell me what makes you so happy."

Marine leant forward,

"Do you remember my speaking of a white light? it was a flame, like that of a candle when there is a, how do you say, a breeze?"

I nodded encouragingly.

"Well, that light or flame, was my spirit, or should I say my higher self, like the trinity. What happened was like so. The flame spoke to me, not with words but directly into my mind, my conscious. It was as though I understood everything about that spirit who was me but not me. I know I have lived many lives and more yet will happen. Alet is my higher self, both separate and yet part of me, but is constantly with me in this life and other lives. Sometimes it was through Alet that I spoke to you and was able to see all that was happening to White Woman Walking, who is also me."

"You are beginning to lose me," I admitted.

"No, it is most simple. You, me, everyone, every living thing has a soul or spirit which lives one life, then another. The higher self is another part, so in each life we are three in one."

"So as you are now, if I understand you correctly, what you are saying is that you are Marine with a soul or spirit that has lived many lives, but as well as those two energies there is a third part to you which you call your higher self, which has the name Alet, but is still you. Marine, and White Woman Walking, as well as several other lives you have had. Alet is constant through each life but your soul changes, evolves as you experience each life."

"Absolutely. I could not have put it better myself," she grinned, obviously pleased to have been understood.

"So what happens in the end?"

"This I cannot answer, except to say I know we come from light, a light which includes every soul and so after who knows how long, we return. It is possible the time for everyone is not the same."

"As for White Woman Walking, was it the fever that ended her life? I ask because I am not clear what happened," I asked, wanting to know more.

"No, indeed not. She recovered, but lost her sight because of the Sun Dance. She lived another fifty years, took a good husband and had five children, four boys and a girl, none of them albino."

"Why should they be albino?" I was again confused.

"Did I not say? I beg your pardon. White Woman Walking was albino, I mean, of course, that it made the Sun Dance all the more painful and dangerous. Perhaps that is another reason for the old man to consider her so brave. It may also answer why she performed the Sun Dance alone, as surely no elder would have sanctioned such a task for an albino."

Later, I saw Marine off at the station. She returned to Edinburgh where she worked as a television producer. I recently received a card from her. She is now living in Canada and enjoys regular treks into the mountains. Interestingly, she has visited Yellowstone Park, to the south of which she found a small town called Thermopolis, which had a yellow mountain with caves and hot springs. She has no doubt that these were the places she remembers from her past life, as she insists that she had never heard of them before.

Luke's Story

Step Back In Time

I was relaxing in 'Hospitality' at Pearson's Television Studio in Stephen Street in the west end of London, with the other participants in a programme about mystics and psychics, when I first met Luke.

The general conversation drifted around the subject matter of the programme and the debate shifted to the issue of reincarnation.

One of the first to put forward her views was Julie Windsor, an attractive woman in her early fifties with glorious silver/blonde hair, made all the more outstanding by her deep tan, expertly applied make-up, long eyelashes and rosy pink lips which matched her talon-like fingernails.

Julie sat forward on the sofa and placed her now empty cup of cappuccino onto a nearby coffee table. She attempted to hitch down the hem of the skirt of her pink suit as he cleared her throat.

"I know all my past lives, of course, as far back as Atlantis where I was a High Priestess", she averred with a confident toss of her silver mane.

"Atlantis! Marvelous! Me too. I remembered being a crystal healer who taught Altantean medicine to the Egyptians,|" interjected Karl Scott-Parker, a five foot four inch rotund, untidy, middle-aged man, whose bright and mismatched clothing starkly contrasted with Julie's elaborately co-ordinated outfit.

"The Egyptians! Marvelous culture of course, but nothing like Atlantis," Karl concluded, running a chubby hand through his thinning hair.

"I have had no experiences", stated Eamon.

Everyone looked in his direction.

"No experiences at all of past lives – but I do believe in them. Then again, I believe in leprechauns and banshees. In fact, I believe in everything – or do I? Who knows?" he finished rather cryptically, puzzling the rest of the room.

He pulled the corners of his mouth down and nodded like a Mafia godfather. Eamon was in his late thirties, although he did not look it, dressed in grey combat pants, zip up trainers and a sloppy jumper, all dressed in the same neutral colour His six foot frame looked muscular under his clothes, his blond hair was long and tied back revealing several piercings in his ears.

"Where do you come from?" Luke asked Eamon.

"Galaway," Eamon replied.

"Can't be that, then. It's just that I have a feeling I have met you before|".

Luke affected the act of being camp to perfection as he enquired. He sat on the edge of the large sofa as he had been from the time of arrival, his knees neatly together with one hand resting over one knee. His long hands were perfectly manicured. He wore a black suit, shirt and immaculately polished black shoes, His fair hair was closely cropped.

Despite looking his age (mid-forties), and his large nose which hooked over his Viva Zapata moustache that looked almost ginger, most people would probably agree he was handsome.

"Maybe you met him in a past life," offered Julie.

Everyone laughed at this.

"That might not be so far from the truth," I put in. "Sometimes when we meet people we get a feeling of familiarity or are sure we have met them before. Also, we meet people and constantly connect or get on like a house on fire. One man I know went on a course and on entering the door saw a woman at the other end of the room and felt an immediate need to go to her side as he felt an ove3rwhelming necessity to protect her.

Alternatively, for no apparent reason, we can feel an intense dislike for someone, even though we know nothing about them. Again, a friend of mine met another woman, a friend of a friend, whom she was assured she would really like as they had such a lot in common. Strangely, my friend took such an intense and irrational dislike to the woman,she actually had a very strong and overwhelming desire to kill her on the spot!

In both cases, the subjects discovered they had respective past lives together which consequently explained these very strong initial feelings. This sixth sense is something we all share." I looked back at everyone. "So what kind of feelings do you have about Eamon, Luke?" I asked.

"I beg your pardon. I'm sure I don't know what you mean," replied Luke, fluttering his eyes in Eamon's direction in an exaggerated manner.

"No, but seriously. The feeling is really quite strong, but is a good positive feeling, not a negative or unpleasant one," Luke added.

Our lively, if a little irreverent debate on past lives came to an end as the studio call came. After the programme recording, we were once again in 'Hospitality', this time waiting for the drivers who would take us to our various destinations. As it turned out, Luke and I travelled in the same car on the short journey to Euston Station. We exchanged business cards before I boarded my train for Liverpool, whilst Luke waited for the train he would take to Manchester.

Six months later, I was dining with my PA, radio presenter Bruno Ecco and his producer, Helen, in a fashionable restaurant off Princess Street in Manchester. The dinner engagement was arranged for the purpose of discussing a new radio programme.

The discussion and meal had just concluded with liqueurs and coffee and we were about to shake hands, when a loud and somewhat inebriated skinhead wearing faded denims, yellow work boots and a white vest with a black leather biker jacket,made a beeline for us. "Raymond, luvvie!" the vision exclaimed in an endearing slur, his arms outstretched.

I was so embarrassed! My cheeks flushed as my PA Clare, her brows raised, mouthed a silent "Who's that?!"

However, fortunately for me, the situation was saved by Bruno who turned to the skinhead and greeted him with, "Luke, baby! I didn't know you and Raymond were acquainted!"

Luke pouted as he hugged first Bruno, then me, before kissing my PA and Helen.

"What do you look like?!" Bruno commented with amusement. "I've just come from Dublin Danny's wake at the Rembrandt, and 'When in Rome' and all that," slurred Luke.

I was lost until Luke explained that Danny was a builder as well as a semi-professional drag queen who had lots of fans amongst the clones (a term for gay men who like to dress in a similar macho way).

It also transpired that Luke was in a long- term relationship with the restaurateur who ran the very restaurant we were patronising, which was in fact co-owned by Luke.

"You must come to our place and help me look at past lives. Would you?" asked Luke.

"Of course, any time at all, "I responded.

"You do that as well as the psychic stuff?" asked Helen. "Of course he does," said Luke, as if he knew all about it. Helen looked at Bruno, then at me.

"We could record it. It would make a great programme for debate". "Oh, I don't know about that," Luke said, shaking his head and suddenly sounding sober.

Notwithstanding, one week later my PA and I arrived at Luke's spacious city centre penthouse apartment. Demitri, Luke's partner opened the door to us. Once inside, the luxury and stylish elegance of the place was truly breathtaking. White walls covered in original works of art gave my PA Clar, (her passion being Fen Shui) a thrill as she spent most of the evening admiring the paintings and sculpture. The floor was the original wood, highly polished and needless to say, all he furniture was the ultimate in designer style.

Bruno and Helen were already waiting with the recording equipment set up, which was a reel to reel tape recorder able to run for several hours. Once switched on everyone except Luke and I left.

Luke, a gifted psychic, had an open mind and so relaxed easily, following the process without any difficulty. Clasping the rose quartz in both hands at his chest, Luke went into the Heart, Light, Harmony State in just a few moments.

I watched as his eyelids showed REM. Then he began to twitch, which in turn led to him thrashing about and mumbling, He had the look of someone in a total nightmare.

I reached across and placed a steadying hand on his forehead. "Be calm.

Calm yourself," I urged him. He let out a weighted sigh then became quite still.

"What do you see?" I asked.

"Fog. A thick fog, but the stench!"

Before Luke could say another work he threw himself forward and retched. He was violently sick. Not surprisingly, this response broke his trance. He rushed into the bathroom.

By the time he returned cleaned and changed, I had already cleaned up the sofa and floor.

"I am sorry about that, but the smell was awful! I have never experienced anything as foul as that before," he volunteered, with some embarrassment.

"I am afraid you had a mild abreaction. It is a physical manifestation caused by an experience whilst in the altered state," I explained.

"Well if that was mild, I wold not care to experience anything stronger than that!" he declared with feeling.

"We may need to abandon the regression session as the same thing is likely to occur again," I warned him.

However, Luke being Luke, he would not hear of it.

"No, it won't. I know what to expect this time," he said positively. "I am not so sure you do. The experience you were having seemed to be very real in its affect on you," I responded dubiously.

"I know. I remember it clearly. I was walking, but my walk was aimless; I was lost and couldn't see anything as the fog and smoke were so thick. The ground was soft and sticky underfoot. I was trudging through mud. I was pulling a great weight behind me, but I don't know what it was. Then into this dense, disorientating atmosphere suddenly drifted noxious odours at once foul, acrid and stinking of putrescence. The very thought of it all makes me nauseous. I can smell it again even now," and his face became distorted into features of disgust.

"Very well. We'll start again, but before we do I will give you a post-hypnotic suggestion so you are not affected by what you see or sense." What do you mean?" asked Luke, obviously puzzled.

"In the Heart, Light, Harmony State you are in a trance, an altered state of awareness. This means I can suggest to you that anything you see or experience will be as though you are viewing it rather than feeling it." This time Luke would be seeing it rather than being actually involved in it.

"! can see the mirror," he began. Then a look of surprise appeared on his face.

"The noise! It is so noisy; terrible, frightening noise! I can't see anything. It is just smoke and noise. That's odd! I heard no noise before nothing. It was as silent as the grave. Now though, the noise is deafening."

As Luke spoke, he became animated, gesticulating with his head, and moving about. Although he was lying on a chaise longue, he energetically writhed and ducked as one might expect of someone playing rugby or running through an assault course.

"The smoke is clearing. Oh my God! The land looks like a quagmire, littered and lousy with bodies of the dead; there are fires doted around. The land slopes down to an open plain, and in the distance I can just make out a black line of cannons and horses; men dressed in dirty, ripped, blue uniforms are becoming clearer now as the smoke is receding and the wind and rain are starting to take its place.

To the left I can see nothing but dead bodies right up to a line of scorched trees where several furtive faces are peering out. It is the same scene behind me and to the right hand side.

A flag has flared open in the wind and rain; momentarily the standard of the blue starred cross on a red background flutters briefly before it falls from the arms of a dying man, who is too obstinate to give up the ghost.

I can see that something is moving up from the mud. It is a figure blurred by the rain swirling around it, but it is becoming obvious that is indeed a man moving towards me. He is dragging something, and that something is another man, a man who for all the world appears totally lifeless. Several other figures are running forward and helping the pair to the cover and safety of the trees.

I am following this haunted and desperate rabble to a clearing behind the tree line where scores of tents are pitched. The body of the lifeless man seems to be just about drawing breath as he is hauled onto a makeshift operating table under canvas. A blood be-spattered surgeon is now examining him.

'He won't last but the hour. I can do nothing here,' the surgeon says. He dismisses the man and moves on to another table to attempt to do what he can with the limited resources available to him.

The surgeon's immediate diagnosis of the other poor wretch is for a double leg amputation above the knee, the feet having being lost in the preceding carnage of the battle that had raged all day but for the moment had halted. The rout that presumable should follow this seems as though it is merely being postponed by the heavy rain. If the rain continues as heavily all day, the chaos might not come at all, these battle weary and pathetic souls might yet live to struggle through another day.

Two orderlies are now beginning to undress the dying man, one pocketing his watch to other using a knife to remove a ring, taking the finger from the left hand as well. The man who was not yet a cadaver now lies naked, mutilated and vulnerable, prey to the vultures both the avian and human variety.

The man who had tried to save his compatriot sits slumped against the wall of the tent, watching the pillaging of his erstwhile comrade without any visible reaction. He has sat there and seen it all, but it does not seem to have registered, or maybe he has seen so much horror that the looting of a dying man now just seemed matter of fact.

As I am watching this harrowing scene, in particular the slumped man, it is dawning on me that I am looking at myself! All of a sudden flashes come to me and I realise his / my name is William trip. I am continuing to watch the vision unfold; a senior officer in a relatively clean uniform of field grey with yellow inlay starts to bawl until he is red in the face. The uniform alone gives his allegiance to the south, his deep southern drawl making him a caricature in what is now becoming clear to me is the American Civil War.

A doctor intervenes; he takes the head of William, the man I recognise as 'me'. Cupping the head in both hands, he turns the face one way then the other. I can see dried blood on the head and at both ears. The doctor looked directly at the officer. "Shout all you want! He won't hear you". Informed the doctor. At that the officer sits down next to William Tripp.

"What have we come to Will?" The officer speaks the words allowed, but seems to be saying them to himself rather than to William. He then places his arm around William and pulls Wills head to his chest. I watch these two men bound together, rock back and forth, both lost in thought, with glazed expressions on their faces."

Luke stopped speaking for a while, evidently deeply affected by what he was reviewing. I waited some five minutes before I prompted him. "Tell me what you see?" I carefully asked Luke. "It's all fading. I can't see so clearly, but I know who the officer is, He is Nathan Ramsbottom, Williams's lifelong friend. I don't know why I didn't recognise him straightaway. We met as lads, when I joined a ship at Bristol. Nat was already an apprentice. He had already been at sea for more than a year. The friendship was instant. He took me under his wing. Nat was fourteen and I was almost thirteen. We eventually left the seafaring life five years later and found work in Georgia in America, far away from England.

Both Nathan and myself succeeded in life, I think mainly because of Nat, and the fact that the ship we served on, had a scholarly first mate who taught both of us to read and write, as well as encouraging in us a good understanding of record keeping and seamanship. Things are coming clearer now. Nathan is still holding William, but William is not for this world. He is stuttering and sighing as he takes a deep breath. He is still and quiet, unable to sit up". Luke opened his eyes "He is dead". I nodded slowly. "Is that it then?" asked Luke "No, there will be more. Lie back, close your eyes and relax". Luke complied and within seconds he was back in REM.

"I am on a ship out at sea, no land in sight, it is a fine day and a good breeze fills the sails. The water is beautiful. I am on the port side. I can see dolphins swimming and cavorting close to the ship. The ship is of the finest timber and well built; all her joints run smoothly and the rigging is tidy, clean and in fine fettle. My, she easily cuts through the gentle waves. All hands are about their business, but I am not the only passenger. There are scores of others all like myself, alone, some looking about the fine vessel, and others just sat or stood about doing nothing, seemingly without a care in the world. They are all smiling, and I suppose I am too as I feel happy, in fact I feel very happy. 'Land ahoy' someone calls out.

Everyone searches in the direction the lookout points to. On the horizon an uneven grey line shrouded in a thin mist comes into view, and then dips below the line of the sea and sky several times, before it comes into a clear focus of green and golds, eventually filling the length of the horizon. 'Paradise!' a voice comes from somewhere behind me." Luke paused then continued to vividly describe the scenario he was revisiting. "I turned around to find a tall strapping man smiling at me, his eyes were sparkling dark brown with large pupils that shone so brightly I could see my own reflection. 'We will land soon he reassured me. His voice was deep and sweet like molasses. 'Will,' I announced my introduction and held out my hand, which to my surprise the man ignored. Instead he simply replied 'I know'. He looked down at my hand, open and ready to shake, but which was now about to drop. He laughed loudly and then threw his arms around me. 'Paradise,' he bawled out through his laughter, whilst his big muscular arms hugged me. By the time he released his grip, the ship had dropped anchor in a lagoon and boats were ferrying people to shore. 'Come,' he urged. 'Do I know you?' I asked, confused by the surroundings. 'Yes, it is just you don't remember.' 'Who are you?' I had to ask. 'What do you mean?' He smiled. 'If you mean my name, it's Samuel.'

'Samuel. I am pleased to meet you.'

'Naturally, and likewise I'm sure. Now shall we go?'

Suddenly I found myself and Samuel being ferried along with others to the shore, for the first time I noticed what I was wearing; the formal dress uniform of a Confederate Lieutenant. The boat was pulled onto the beach with the help of men who reminded me of a Polynesian I had once met, and like him they were marked with Moko (the Maori word for tattoo), with intricate patterns on their faces and bodies.

I stepped out onto a golden sandy beach which was crowded with people like me arriving from not just one ship, but many. I stood for a moment looking about me. The sky was clear blue apart for half a dozen small clouds, the sun being at a point half way between the land and apex of the sky. Beyond the beach trees and shrubs blazoned every shade of green and purple supporting numerous flowers of red and yellow, the like of which I had never set eyes upon before. Beyond the trees rose a mountain so high in places that snow topped some of the peaks, and from one coned shaped mountain in the far distance the summit smoked with wisps so typical of a volcano, alive and active, but not yet rumbling with anger.

Samuel took my arm to lead me, and I was aware of his grip.

'I want some answers. First, where are we? What am I doing here? Who are all these people?' I demanded, wanting to comprehend what exactly I was part of.

'Pa-ra-dies,' he broke up the word as he said it, singing each syllable.

'What does that mean? I don't ...' I did not finish the sentence, as for the first time it dawned on me that none of this could be possible. It must surely be a dream, I thought to myself. I must be delirious, yes, that's it. The last thing I remember was being in a battle and I was hurt. I had not been able to hear anything clearly, but I had been in pain. My head hurt I had been trudging through mud, dragging a man back to the field hospital. Everyone had been dead or dying. I looked at Samuel.

'It's a dream. I am delirious in a fever on some hospital bed. This and you are all in my imaginings,' I reasoned.

'Is that so?' he raised his eyebrows. 'Well then, let's see where your imaginings take us.'

I looked to the trees and shrubs and I could see all the others disappearing into them. I looked back and the last of the ships was leaving the lagoon and the ferry boats were nowhere to be seen. Samuel lead and I followed as we trudged through fern, bush and tropical forest. The air was full of bird song. Occasionally chimps and monkeys could be seen high in the branches. Also the buzz and hum of numerous exotic insects joined in with the melody of life in this beautiful place, which also gave home to the most exotic and colourful flora. From time to time I would stop to take in the scent and aromas of the intoxicatingly beautiful flowers. My lazy meandering caused no concern to Samuel, he just marched on. I almost lost sight of him, and so had to run to catch up with him. By the time I reached him we had cleared the wooded area and had arrived in an open grassland in which beast were roaming; gazelles, buffalo and lions oddly all at peace in their mingling with each other and with us. The volcano I had seen earlier now dominated the landscape as it rose up before us.

'Are you for the climb?' enquired Samuel with the brightest of smiles.

'Lead on,' I answered as it dawned on me that what was unfolding would happen despite me, or as Samuel implied because of me. We began to ascend the climb was gentle and easy to walk. Each step kicked up clouds of pale grey pumice. Occasionally, sharp, jet black pieces of obsidian glistened and shimmered, reflecting the sun light. It should have been hot on such a sunny day and warm under foot on this smoking volcano, but it was not, it was just comfortable.

Before we reach the summit, the rim of this fine mountain, we came to a plateau. It felt as if we were half way up. I looked back. To my astonishment I could see nothing but sky and below us the clouds obliterated our view of the place we had travelled from.

'How far have we come, how high are we, I don't remember clouds?' I asked somewhat baffled.

'Far enough for now, we will rest awhile in there,' Samuel pointed in the direction of a cave close by that I had not noticed.

Once inside, what I saw took my breath away. It was to all intents and purposes like the lobby of a luxurious five star hotel, well lit by crystal chandeliers. The floor was the finest in opulent terrazzo and the walls were of marble. There were a seemingly endless number of occasional tables dotted around and these in turn were surrounded by easy chairs, all of which were occupied. In addition a great number of people were also standing around. Some were deep in conversation with each other whilst others seemed to be alone and were silent.

Slowly a realisation came to me. This elegant place that stretched as far as i could see in every direction was impossibility. We had stepped into a cave on the side of a volcano, on an island with a rain forest which included every type of life I knew, but also life I did not know, nor indeed had ever dreamt about.

'Paradise' Samuel had said, paradise and a little more. Then I remembered about the journey on the ship, the ferry across the lagoon. My mind raced. I am dead! I thought, I am amongst the dead! I began to tremble.

'Samuel, Samuel!' I shouted out his name.

I was in panic, but he was close at my side. 'You have no need to shout, I can hear you well enough.' He put a finger to his lips and hushed me.

'Come with me to the library, you need to know yourself, then we will see what you are to do'.

'What do you mean?' I asked, still bemuse and apprehensive.

Again he hushed me with a finger to his lips. We came to a marble staircase which swept upward. I followed Samuel. At last we reach the entrance of the library. Two large and beautiful walnut doors swung open into the library, which was surprisingly small and contained no books. It was a plain white marble room, about twelve feet square. The marble glowed pure white without any veins, so the whiteness was absolute. In the centre, a raised dais of walnut supported a font carved in the shape of a simple chalice, also of the same white marble.

Samuel took my hand and led me to the font which was almost full of the cleanest, purest water. Without Samuel speaking, I knew what to do. I cupped my hands and drank greedily from the font. It was the most refreshing water I had ever tasted. In that refreshment I felt well, so well in fact I can't remember ever feeling better.

Suddenly thunder roared, the escalating vibrations threw me around the room. I clung to the font. The vibration subsided, but the water continued to ripple in small circular waves, outwards from its centre. As I watched mesmerised by the rippling water, a vision appeared. I could see a woman giving birth. I realised it was my birth as I stood there my whole life unfolded in front of me. All was displayed in the rippling water of the font. It was all there – my birth into poverty and squalor, to a mother who died within days of my coming into the world. A father who abandoned me, leaving me with his elder sister, who did her best to raise my amongst her own brood of nine.

Hunger and want was all I knew in my childhood, as a youth I went to sea and was able to work my way through continued hardship onto success, a far cry from my humble beginnings in a Lancashire town and onto becoming a land owner in Georgia. I had lived a rich, gentleman's life, blessed with a loving wife, Katie, and two adorable and adoring children. Then I spoke out, 'Katie, will I ever see you again?' The words tumbled out. For the first time since entering Samuel's paradise I felt lost, pain and loneliness. I cried. The faces of Katie and my children and all I had lost filled my head. My body shook with enormous sobs as tears rolled hot and wet from my cheeks and fell into the font. As soon as the tears mixed with the pure crystal clear water, steam began to rise and the water boiled away, leaving the font quite dry, much to my astonishment.

'What's happening?' I asked Samuel, completely fascinated and bewildered.

'Only knowledge,' he replied cryptically. 'Soon you will understand.'

'I wish so much that I was with my family,' I continued heartbroken. As I spoke them, my words were deeply earnest. Instantly I was back in Georgia, on my plantation walking to my home, except the once beautiful mansion was no more, it had become just a burnt out shell and my surrounding land despoiled.

'What is this?' I stammered my emotions raw as I bellowed out the demand.

'Don't fret! Your family is safe and sound. It is to be many years before they leave this world, but come, you can see them,' reassured Samuel.

I was still burning with rage and yet impotency.

'This war! What was it all for, why do we come to arms so easily? I don't even know what it was all about any more!'

I looked at Samuel and for the first time I realised he was a black man, and I had never in all my life spent time in conversation with anyone black before. The only dealings I had with them previously was perhaps to give them orders in place of the overseer, but that had always been without even a thought as to the human face of these toilers. Nor had I ever seen the need to question the morals of paying white men that might have sold their labour, whilst at the same time owning and doing as I liked with the black people, whom I thought no more of than any of my live stock, and maybe less of them than my precious horses.

'Are you an angel, or the devil's advocate? What would you do with me?' I asked fearfully.

'What would you have me do with you?' He flatly retorted.

'Take me to my wife and children. Let me speak with them one last time,' I begged.

'Certainly I will take you there. But as for speaking to them, well I cannot help you there.'

Before I knew it I was in the house of a neighbour, and by God's grace, I could see my wife. Although I was shocked to see her looking so thin and pale, I could still discern the inner strength I knew she possessed and had been one of the qualities that had drawn me to her in the first place.

She was in the act of chastising our boy Jonathan. Samuel had been true to his word my family were safe and well.

'Boys will be boys!' Elizabeth Grady, the wife of one of our neighbours, was saying. I think she was trying to ease Katie's discomfort. I guessed she was feeling my wife's anxiety, even though it was unfounded. Thomas Grady and his wife Elizabeth were good kinfolk, and saw no barrier in welcoming my family into their household. I looked around at Thomas's house. It had once been described as one of the most elegant house in all the Americas. Now, however, the walls were bare, there were no carpets, only scuffed boards. The windows were free from drapes and the absence of furniture seemed to enlarge the mansion even more, giving it a desolate air. Every sound echoed in the new austerity of a once rich home.

I turned to Samuel, 'Will Thomas survive the war or will he lose all?' I ventured to ask, hopping he would have the answer.

I held my breath for a few moments, perhaps dredging the answer.

'The war is over, but as to the future I cannot say, but for now these people are beginning to build it again.'

Samuel had what I think was a kind expression on his face as he spoke.

'We must go now William,' he sighed.

'Not yet. I want to hold my wife. I want to kiss her and my boy and girl,' I pleaded.

Samuel's voice became firm, 'You are no longer flesh and blood, Will, so what you wish is not possible.'

Despite Samuel's decisive objection, I went to Katie. She was standing at a window looking out as Eva was playing with her brother and the other children. I put my arm around her, but I could feel no substance.

It made me inconsolably sad; I wanted to cry and though i knew it was futile I kissed Katie's neck at the nape, as from habit. Samuel coughed an interruption. I stepped away and in that same instant, Katie shivered and held herself.

'I do miss you Will.' She whispered, with a tremor in her voice.

It absolutely broke my heart to hear it and to see her so disconsolate. 'She felt that!' I exclaimed, turning to Samuel with tears brimming.

'Yes I believe she did, but come now, we must be away,' he urged.

I found myself back on the side of the volcano in the blinking of an eye. Again, Samuel led me into the cave and once again we were in the foyer full of people milling about.

'Who are these people?' I asked, now somewhat bemused.

'Just weary souls,' responded Samuel.

'Well, are they like me, dead waiting for judgment?'

'No, no, no. Anyway, it is your business we are concerned with, not other souls. Now, come!'

We entered a corridor that had steps leading gently downwards. The walls glowed a golden orange. There were no doors along the corridor and it seemed to run in a long straight line. The corridor opened into a spacious domed room, which, however not as light and bright as the corridor. It took a little while for my eyes to adjust to the new dimmer light. Standing in the centre of the room and looking around, I could see a further eleven corridors leading of this domed chamber.

But there was another source of light in the chamber which came in the form of a fire in the centre which rose out of a well in the floor. We approached the flame. I could see the behaved like no other fire I had ever experienced. The well was about a yard in diameter, and the flame kept to its shape as it rose up through this and continued up to the ceiling of the dome. It seemed as though an invisible force kept the fire going in the yard wide pillar, which oddly enough gave out very little heat as I stood with Samuel gazing into orange, red and blue flames.' What is this?' I asked Samuel now intensely curious.

'Life,' he said quite simply. 'It is now time for you to judge,' he announced.

'I do not understand..What do you mean 'judge?' I replied with a question. I was mystified. The sense of panic which had subsided began to surface again.

'Have you not lived your life?' asked Samuel.

'Ye-es,' I carefully answered, but was puzzled by the rhetorical question.

'Think about what you feel. Think about what you have done. Think about how others have treated you, think about how you have treated others, and think about what you have yet to do,' and with that Samuel left.

Suddenly I felt extreme loneliness. I missed Katie. I thought of her and how much I still love her. My thoughts drifted back to where we had first met. We had both been at a party at the Hogan's estate. I was still learning to be a gentleman, but my rough edges still showed through. Despite my clumsiness it was love at first sight for both of us, and with the help of George Hogan we had started courting, marrying within two years.

Then came Jonathan and Eva, our precious children who had such a life – good and wholesome, and God – fearing, unlike me who was nothing but a scallywag. As I stood there alone, facing the flame, my loneliness became more acute. Was I an honourable man? I asked myself. I had to admit the answer was no. Then I became ashamed as i remembered all the lying, cheating and deception I had been guilty of in the name business. I had justified my actions always, even though I knew I was making my life so good, it always seemed to be at the expense of others' misfortune. The realisation hit me. I had gone to war for no good reason. It was pride alone. My friends and neighbours were all fired up about a belief in what they considered a right. They were fighting for a way of life, a belief in themselves, autonomy and the right not to be governed from afar. I had no noble motive, just a foolish wish to conform, to be like the others and keep my safe, protected way of life.

'Samuel!' I cried out his name.

'What can I do for you, William?' he was still near.

'Why you? Why are you my, my helper ... angel ..exactly what are you' I demanded.

'I am what you make me,' Samuel responded vaguely.

'But what does that mean? If I was to create an angel it would have wings and be like the angels in paintings, not the way you are.' I felt extremely puzzled.

He replied in the same obscure vain as earlier. 'I am only as you would have me, no more, no less. If my colour offends you, I cannot help that. It is how you see me.'

Quickly I responded, 'Why should I be offended? It is just, well there is your kind, and there is mine ... 'I offered.

'But I am no kind'. I am, I repeat, what you make me. Without you I do not exist,' he responded enigmatically.

'Enough of these digressions. I know my fate. I am not for heaven. I am for torment for all time.' I was becoming agitated.

'But why so Will?'

'Do you really need to ask? How you mock me. I am weak and full of sin. I cannot go to heaven or paradise as you call it.'

'Why not? What stops you? Your place here in paradise is ready for you,' said Samuel sagely.

'No I am not worthy. Only if I had a chance to do it all over again, I would and I would do it properly,' I said with conviction.

'Are you suggesting you did not do it properly this time then?' He asked, appearing slightly amused. 'No I certainly did not, but next time I now know what I should do,' I responded with feeling.

I am sorry, Will, but it is not quite as easy as it might seem. You can return and live another life, but you would have no knowledge of you previous life, or of the afterlife either. You would be innocent.'

'Then send me back. Let me start again, so I may repent, and meet my Katie again, so we can start over,' I was becoming increasingly desperate now.

'Ah, um – it is not quite what you are thinking. We cannot turn back the clock. That life is over. I think I can show you what I mean.'

Samuel stepped forward into the strange flame. In that moment I panicked. I feared he would burn. He did not, but instead he slowly began to ascend inside the pillar of fire.

'Come with me, there is nothing to fear,' he urged.

With more than a little anxiety, I took all my courage and followed my guide's lead. Hesitantly at first, I tentatively reached out my hand and placed it into the centre of the flame. I almost pulled back as tingles of pins and needles ran over my skin. Faith in Samuel helped me immerse myself totally inside the flame. Once inside, a wonderful feeling came over me. I was weightless, and the tingling stopped as I rose higher and higher out through the top of the dome and into a starry sky.

Then we both floated into the night air flying like birds on the wing, all the time rising higher and higher until we were so high the land below looked like pictures in an atlas. It was the most fantastic feeling as i could see the whole earth below me turning and spinning through the havens. I was able to see the sun and moon at the same time.

Then we stopped, just Samuel and I alone in space, just us two beings facing each other amongst the sun, moon and stars seemingly all alone in the universe.

'Are you ready for paradise, or do you want to go back?' He nodded toward earth as he posed the question. I followed the direction of his gaze and saw how beautiful the world looked. I recalled all the horror and desolation that had ended my life along with many thousands more, and thought with sorrow of all those widows and orphans. How could such a beautiful blue green jewel be so infected with pain, sorrow and suffering? I had been unconcerned about other people, so matter-of-fact about having slaves drawn into my service. With all this in my mind, I asked a question of Samuel; though I feared the answer he might give.

'If I go back to the world, what kind of life will I have? Will I pay dearly for my misdeeds?'

'No,' he said quite simply.

'No! That's it? No' I exclaimed.

'Well,' continued Samuel, 'I only mean you will choose a life, there is no penance, no recompense. Maybe think about what you need to learn and understand to set you free, so you may go on to Paradise.'

'But how will i do that?' I asked genuinely puzzled.

'Look,' and as he said the word he waved his arm and images of people come into view. I could see and hear them clearly as though I was in the room with them. I do not know how much time passed, but it seemed in a twinkling I had been shown many, many people all different, all from different countries and speaking every language, though amazingly, I was able to understand them all. 'I cannot choose. What do you think, Samuel?'

'Oh, it is not for me or anyone else to choose. You must decide this for yourself.'

'But how do I know what is the right life for me?' I asked with concern.

'Be assured you will know,' answered Samuel wisely. Before he finished speaking, something caught my eye. It was a lovely gentle face. It belong to a woman who looked kind; she was smiling as she walked hand in hand with a man. He looked equally happy.

'Who are they?' I asked Samuel.

'Well let me see,' he closed his eyes for a moment, then a tremendous smile came over his face. 'Oh, yes. Oh, yes!' he exclaimed.

'Why, what is it?' I asked, not knowing to be alarmed or excited.

'Do you think you would like them as parents?' Samuel asked with a smile in his voice.

'Oh, why, yes, I do believe I would. Yes,' I responded with enthusiasm.

'Good, without a doubt you will learn a lot in the life these parents would give you.'

'Is that good – for me I mean?' I enquired.

'Come, come,' said Samuel, 'there is someone you need to meet,' and with that we found ourselves standing in a room full of white light so bright that nothing of the room itself could be seen. Then for the first time I was aware of another presence standing alongside Samuel and myself. Samuel took my hand and placed it in the hand of the other. As we started to talk, an extreme sense of joy came over me."

Luke stopped speaking. He sighed, and then opened his eyes which were moist. Sighing again, he sat up and put his head in his hands. I watch him for no more than a minute, when he got up.

"Excuse me," he choked, walking past me to the bathroom to wash his face. He then strolled back towel in hand.

"I met my twin," he announced.

"Sorry. What was that?" I asked, thinking I had misheard him.

"Before I entered the womb I held the hand of my twin sister. We went together, we supported each other, even before we were born."

"I hadn't realised you were a twin," I remarked with surprise.

"Yes and of course, we are very close, even though she lives in London. We talk all the time on the phone."

"So you remember being in the womb?" I tried not to sound too excited.

"Yes. What a wonderful place it was. It was not as dark as you might imagine. We could see each other and communicate; it must have been a kind of telepathy. I could also hear everything outside, but inside it was beautiful, the sounds that surrounded ourselves in there were so comforting and beautiful and the beat so soothing."

Luke sat back on the sofa and looked me in the eye.

"That's it. Nothing else. No, wait, there is something else, I remember.

All the time our mother was pregnant with me and Sue, a record over and over." He bit his lip with the memory in his head, his foot tapping as the tune swam through his mind. Then he jumped up and began to sing Tower of Strength, Laughingly mimicking the fifties crooner Frankie Vaughan (the singer who made the song famous).

A short while after this we left the penthouse and went to meet our friends at the restaurant with a very interesting tape recording of Luke's past life and womb memories.

When I left Luke that evening he was still brimming with excitement. He told me he could not wait until the following morning when he would phone his twin sister and tell her all.

Later the next day I received a call from Luke, who enthusiastically informed me of a phone call he had received from his twin sister, Susan. It seemed that before he had the chance to tell her all about the fantastic revelations which had transpired the previous night, she told him about a very strange dream she just had about being in the womb!

Epilogue

No matter what we do, or what we believe in, each of us carries responsibility for our own souls, as well as maybe also for those of others.

I deeply believe that if we do not learn lessons in or form a past existence, then we are destined to live as many lives as necessary until we attain a state of spiritual grace and achieve the blissful state of Nirvana.

It is interesting to note that in my experience, each time a past life is examined, individuals seem to remember an afterlife which is appropriate to their culture or beliefs. Possibly this is necessary for the soul's ultimate transit to the spirit world, and perhaps we will never really know what our final destination is to be, until we arrive there.

17751432R00128

Printed in Poland
by Amazon Fulfillment
Poland Sp. z o.o., Wrocław